THE GREATEST BATMAN STORIES EVER TOLD

VOLUME 2

BATMAN CREATED BY BOB KANE

WARNER BOOKS

THE GREATEST BATMAN STORIES EVER TOLD VOLUME TWO
All stories previously published by DC Comics Inc. 1940, 1941, 1953,
1954, 1965, 1967, 1974, 1977, 1982, 1983, 1986, 1987. Compilation
and covers © 1992 DC Comics Inc. All Rights Reserved. Batman and
all related characters, their distinctive likenesses and related indicia are
trademarks of DC Comics Inc. All Rights Reserved. The stories, characters, and incidents featured in this publication are entirely fictional.

ISBN 0-446-39427-0

Published by arrangement with DC Comics Inc.,
1325 Avenue of the Americas, New York, NY 10019
Warner Books, Inc., 1271 Avenue of the Americas, New York, NY 10020
Ⓦ A Time Warner Company
Printed in Canada.
First Warner Printing July 1992

Cover illustration by Eduardo Barreto and Les Dorscheid
Publication design by Dale Crain

This volume is dedicated to the spirit of the Golden Age of comics, which enabled a Bat-Man to protect the city from grotesque villains such as The Penguin or deadly antagonists as The Cat.

TABLE OF CONTENTS

6   **INTRODUCTION**
by Martin Pasko

12   **FOREWORD**
by Mike Gold

15   **THE CAT**
Originally presented in BATMAN #1 (Spring 1940)

28   **ONE OF THE MOST PERFECT FRAME-UPS"**
Originally presented in DETECTIVE COMICS #58 (Dec. 1941)

41   THE SECRET LIFE OF CATWOMAN
Originally presented in BATMAN #62 (Dec. 1950-Jan. 1951)

53   THE PENGUINS' FABULOUS FOWLS
Originally presented in BATMAN #76 (Apr.-May 1953)

63   CRIMES OF THE CATWOMAN
Originally presented in DETECTIVE COMICS #203 (Jan. 1954)

75   PARTNERS IN PLUNDER
Originally presented in BATMAN #169 (Feb. 1965)

89   THE PENGUIN TAKES A FLYER INTO THE FUTURE
Originally presented in BATMAN #190 (Mar. 1967)

112   CATWOMAN SETS HER CLAWS FOR BATMAN
Originally presented in BATMAN #197 (Dec. 1967)

135   HAIL EMPEROR PENGUIN
Originally presented in BATMAN #257 (Jul.-Aug. 1974)

155   THE MALAY PENGUIN
Originally presented in DETECTIVE COMICS #473 (Nov. 1977)

172   CATWOMAN FEATURETTE
Originally presented in BATMAN #256 (May-Jun. 1974)

173   TERROR TRAIN
Originally presented in BATMAN #345 (Mar. 1982)

180   IN THE LAND OF THE DEAD
Originally presented in BATMAN #346 (Apr. 1982)

187   NEVER SCRATCH A CAT
Originally presented in BATMAN #355 (Jan. 1983)

210   PENGUIN FEATURETTE
Originally presented in BATMAN #257 (Jul.-Aug. 1974)

212   LOVE BIRDS
Originally presented in BATMAN ANNUAL #11 (1987)

227   EYRIE
Originally presented in DETECTIVE COMICS #568 (Nov. 1986)

249   END NOTES
by Robert Greenberger

253   BIOGRAPHIES
by Paul Kupperberg

OF FOWLS AND FELINES: FIFTY YEARS OF FELONY

By Martin Pasko

Not too long ago, a Warner Bros. executive addressing a large gathering spoke of how certain media had proclaimed 1990 The Year of the Bat, and he assured those media that 1992 would be an even bigger year for the Dark Knight. He then lovingly recalled, to hearty laughter from the crowd, the syndicated gag-cartoon panel about a TV news crew gathering on the front lawn of the only man in America who didn't own a Batman T-shirt.

So it would come as no surprise to me if by now you're so accustomed to seeing the Batman all over the place—on screens large and small, on billboards and in shop windows everywhere—that it's easy to forget: the Batman is not just *in* the comics, he is *of* the comics. Always has been, and probably always will be—a fair statement, I think, considering he's been published in that form continuously for almost 53 years.

As I listened to the gentleman from Warners speak, I couldn't help but feel a distinct jolt of *déjà vu*. Because we've been through all this before, ladies and gentlemen —though the first time it was on a somewhat smaller, and certainly sillier, scale.

In any event, we are living during the third period in the history of popular culture when the world has been seized by a paroxysm of Bat-mania. Which is why I don't need to acquaint you with this character.

I don't need to tell you that the hero created in 1939 by artist Bob Kane, with an assist from writer Bill Finger, is, unlike the many superpowered colleagues who followed him onto brightly colored comic-book pages, a mortal crimefighter who struggles and triumphs in the dark places. Not just the shadowy alleys and back streets of a sprawling city at night, but the Stygian corners of his own tortured soul.

I don't have to explain that he has conditioned himself to the peak of physical perfection and is arguably the world's greatest detective, as well as a brilliant scientist and inventor and a master of the martial arts. I needn't remind you that he has dedicated himself to developing those skills and abilities with but one purpose—to fulfill a vow made at the graves of his parents—and in so doing, to cleanse his city of its rot of crime and corruption.

BRIAN STELFREEZE

Nor must I tell you that his vow was to avenge his parents, whose murder by a gunman's bullets in an alley when he was but eight years old changed the course of his life irrevocably. I don't need to say that in the crucible of that alley was forged an ineluctable avenging force. A masked and cloaked vigilante. "A creature of the night," as the world first learned in the pages of DETECTIVE COMICS #33, "black and terrible," that would strike terror into the hearts of the "superstitious and cowardly lot" of criminals he would face in the five decades to come.

The first time the awareness of these same facts was shared by most of the population of the planet was a little more than twenty-five years ago. And it is to memories of this time that I return each time I hear that term "Bat-mania." I can't describe the feeling as nostalgia; that word is reserved for memories bathed in a glow of contentment. But I, like many other preteens who were deeply into comic books at the time, quickly learned to loathe a mass-medium incarnation of one of our favorite comics characters—one that, as *Batman* editor Denny O'Neil has so rightly put it, "turned the character into a comedian."

Still, we remember the winter of 1966 as if it were yesterday, precisely because it was the year our worlds were suddenly rendered in the bold primary colors and spare, emphatic lines of the comic art form. For, on television, Batman stormed the beachheads of the pop-cultural landscape with an overnight smash-hit series. The show transposed intact the formal elements and conventions of the *Batman* comics to the film medium, where their ludicrous, jarring inappropriateness elicited laughter and gave the culture a definition of the neologism "camp" that was far more cogent than any Susan Sontag could provide.

It would be quite some time before anyone would again see the grim, mysterious hard-boiled detective-by-night that had been created by Kane in 1939 and, forty-six years later, would be reinvented by Frank Miller as The Dark Knight.

The TV series would, however, introduce an entire generation to an element of the mythology that had never been seen in any previous mass-medium version of the character. There had been no budget for it when the Batman was the star of two howlingly low-budget Columbia serials, in 1943 and 1949 respectively. Nor was there time, in 15-minute adventures, to explore this aspect of the character when he was heard on radio in the mid-1940's, as a guest star on *The Adventures of Superman* (in the person of Gary Merrill, later more famous as Bette Davis's husband and co-star in *All About Eve*). And it was a dimension of the Batman that had been largely missing from the comics, due primarily to shifts in popular taste, for roughly fifteen years.

I am of course referring to the inimitable "Rogues Gallery" of costumed villains.

Thanks to the television series, those colorful characters are as inextricably linked in the public imagination to the Batman character as Robin the erstwhile Boy Wonder or Alfred the butler. So it seemed only natural, after Jack Nicholson's fascinatingly perverse interpretation of The Joker in the first *Batman* theatrical feature, that director Tim Burton and his producers would choose to similarly revitalize the next two heavy hitters in this pantheon of villainy, The Penguin and The Catwoman —in the persons of Danny DeVito and Michelle Pfeiffer—in *Batman Returns*. Which in turn makes it only natural that DC's editorial board would choose to make the felonious fowl and feline the focus of this, the second collection of the greatest Batman stories ever told.

For me, the stories in this volume are old friends, to whom I'd recently been reintroduced in the course of doing research for Warner Bros. Animation's forthcoming *Batman—The Animated Series*, on which I'm delighted to be working as a writer/story editor. For obvious reasons, The Penguin and The Catwoman will appear in many of the half-hour adventures that begin airing weekdays in September of 1992 on the Fox network, beautifully rendered by some

of the best animators in the field and delightfully voiced by Paul Williams and Adrienne Barbeau.

And so, during a recent visit to New York to search the vast DC archives for stories that might inspire our writers, I was approached by editor Mike Gold to provide this introduction. I found it not only informative, but even more fun than I remembered, to be able to track the development of these characters from their inception as I reread the stories contained herein.

While the various chronicles of the history of comic books are filled with fascinating firsthand accounts of how several of the *Batman* Rogues Gallery were created, there doesn't seem to be a consensus on where The Catwoman came from. That's probably because, unlike such villains as The Joker, The Scarecrow, or Two-Face, who over the years remained largely unchanged from their first, full-blown appearances, The Catwoman slowly *evolved*. And, as such inventive writers as Frank Miller, Mindy Newell, and Alan Grant, and such dazzlingly talented illustrators as David Mazzucchelli, J. J. Birch, Michael Bair, and Norm Breyfogle have demonstrated most recently, The Catwoman remains one of the most frequently redesigned and reinterpreted characters in the Batman mythology.

In her earliest appearances, she looked as she does in the first story in this volume, reprinted from BATMAN #1: an exotically beautiful, dark-haired young woman in a vaguely Oriental-looking dress. As you will see, in her debut she is quite specifically a jewel thief—a "cat burglar." There is no indication that her creators had even an inkling of the cat-o'-nine-tails, claw-like weapons, cat-shaped equipment, or feline-themed crimes that would later become her trademarks.

Even her name kept changing. She isn't even The Catwoman in her first appearance—merely "The Cat." Perhaps sensing that there was further work to be done, Kane and company returned to the drawing board immediately, and the character reappeared in the

JIM APARO

DAVE STEVENS

found the inspiration for The Joker in a deck of playing cards, writer Bill Finger has shared with comics historians his recollection of how he created the character that came to be known, in the days when the floridly-phrased caption was in vogue, as the Bold Bird of Banditry, the Buccaneer of Birds, or The Man of A Thousand Umbrellas.

As one might suspect from Bob Kane's many, often wildly disparate accounts of how the Batman himself was invented (For, what storyteller can resist a good yarn? And when they ask you where you get your ideas, you have to tell them *something*), Finger's account might well be apocryphal. But, as he told it, in 1940 he was smoking a certain brand of Menthol cigarette whose trademark was a little cartoon penguin. One day while casting about for a story premise, he happened to glance down at the pack and found there the genesis of the second story reprinted in this collection, "One of the Most Perfect Frame-Ups."

Unlike The Catwoman, who made half a dozen appearances before hitting on the purple peek-a-boo-skirted costume and "purr-fidious" M.O. that ultimately defined the character, most of the familiar Penguin trademarks are in evidence in this story from DETECTIVE #58: the beak-like nose, swallowtail coat, monocle, top hat, cigarette-holder, and umbrella—they're all there.

As are the love of fine art, the taste for Shakespeare, and even a hint of the pompous, overblown manner of speech that would, in The Penguin's next appearance, take on a more indentifiably British flavor. Even the concept of his vast array of trick-umbrella weapons premiered at the same time he did, as you'll notice by the bullets, gas, and acid that his parasol dispenses in the first story alone.

Yet the conception of the character is just as clearly embryonic. Not yet in evidence, for example, is the Penguin's predilection for crimes using birds as weapons or planned around avian themes. This gimmick would not come into play until DETECTIVE #62 (Sept., 1942), in the story called "Crime's Early Bird." And in his first few

next two issues of BATMAN, referred to variously as the Cat Woman and the Cat-Woman. It wasn't until the mid-1940's that everyone seems to have settled on the simpler "Catwoman."

There was no such ambiguity, nor any similar mutability, about the rogue who took his first bow in the story beginning on page 28. Within a year of creating their slinky jewel thief, Kane, Finger, and Kane's assistant, illustrator Jerry Robinson—by now joined by inker George Roussos—would come up with a third distinctive adversary for their bat-cloaked hero. And the new villain would temporarily eclipse The Cat-Woman in popularity, if number of encores is any indication.

The pudgy, waddling, criminal connoisseur of the finer things in life, whose given name of Oswald Cobblepot would not be invented for at least another thirty years, returned in some thirty-three *Batman* adventures over the next quarter-century (thirty-*four* if you count a 1946 Sunday continuity for the *Batman* syndicated newspaper strip, reprinted in the first volume in this series). All this before 1966, when he began to enjoy an even greater notoriety thanks to the TV series.

The creation of this character, who in the 1940's became, after The Joker, the second most-frequently-appearing Batman villain, is just about the only positive thing I can think of ever having come from cigarette smoking. Just as Robinson has told of having appearances, The Penguin is quite clearly a cold-blooded murderer, rather than the comparatively benign bandit he later became. By the time he first met The Joker in the mid-40's ("Knights of Knavery," reprinted in the first volume), he seemed content to concentrate on theft, and by "The Riddle of the Seven Birds" in BATMAN #56 (Dec. 1949-Jan. 1950), he is described as a felon who has "never killed anybody."

By the early 1950's, when the Penguin was settling for terrorizing Gotham with mechanical mythical beasts (our fourth golden oldie, "The Penguin's Fabulous Fowls"), The Catwoman had finally become the character she is today—more or less. After four appearances wearing a costume topped by a grotesque cat's-head mask, and assuming a variety of aliases such as Marguerite Tone and Elva Barr, The Catwoman finally emerged in 1946 (in "Nine Live Has the Catwoman, " in BATMAN #35) in the cat-eared cowl that would remain her definitive appearance well into the next decade. But she hadn't stopped changing her hair color; she is blonde in the 1946 tale, after having appeared both as a sultry brunette and a raven-haired temptress.

In "The Secret Life of the Catwoman" (reprinted here), we first learned that her real name was Selina Kyle, and that she was the daughter of a pet shop owner when she lost her memory due to an injury sustained in a plane crash. When a blow to the head cured her amnesia, she renounced her criminal past and settled down to a quiet life as Selina Kyle, proprietor of (what else?) a pet shop...and of a still-unrequited love for the cowled crusader. It is from this retirement that she is goaded into emerging by the city's scorn in the 1954 story, "The Crimes of the Catwoman" replete with cat-signal, refitted kitty-car, and catboat.

The late 50's and early 60's are unrepresented in this volume, having spawned a Batman that was, in its way, even more surreal than the TV show to come. Those were the days of the impossibly square-jawed Batman and fey, spit-curled

Robin, who were always shown in these arms-akimbo poses that made them less resemble human beings than bendable "action figures." These are the Batman and Robin who were always meeting pointy-eared "aliens from outer space," whose heads seemed to be drawn by tracing bowling balls and who came in almost as many colors as a Princess telephone.

During this period, Catwoman disappeared altogether—replaced for a time by an orange-and-yellow humanoid tabby imaginatively dubbed Cat-Man—and The Penguin made but two appearances, one in 1956 and another in 1963.

Already The Penguin's decline in stature, to that of a character you could never quite take seriously, had begun—a situation not helped by the scenery-chewing of Burgess Meredith in the TV series. As a kind of cultural artifact, we've included two Penguin tales from that period, during which editor Julius Schwartz, veteran writers like John Broome, Gardner Fox, and Ed Herron, and gifted artists like Sheldon Moldoff, Joe Giella, and (usually on covers) Carmine Infantino labored heroically to bring some of the old dignity back to this by-now rather silly buffoon.

In the mid-70's, Denny O'Neil, Irv Novick and Dick Giordano succeeded admirably as well, in "Hail Emperor Penguin," setting the stage for the brilliant writer-artist team of Steve Englehart and Marshall Rogers to recast the character as a formidable adversary in their memorable "Malay Penguin." Their lead was followed in the subsequent writing of Doug Moench, Joey Cavalieri, and Max Allan Collins, and the dynamic graphics of talents like Gene Colan, Klaus Janson, and the aforementioned Mr. Breyfogle, whose efforts from the 1980s under editors Len Wein and Denny O'Neil round out our collection. The tradition reestablished in that work continues today.

The Catwoman, too, was ill-served by television, beginning with a costume redesign—replicated in "Catwoman Sets Her Claws for Batman"—featuring something that looked like a cross between an overgrown domino mask and harlequin glasses, which had the

unfortunate effect of making Julie Newmar's head look like the back of a '61 Biscayne. Numerous redesigns and reinterpretations of the character followed; one by Frank Robbins can be seen herein, in the featurette from 1974. But in the early 80's under editor Wein, The Catwoman returned briefly to her old, classic self, until the Miller-Mazzucchelli incarnation that debuted in the BATMAN: YEAR ONE series could set the standard of excellence that ushered the character into the 90's.

What lasting impact on the Batman mythology will be made by the big-screen versions of these characters served up by Batman Returns remains to be seen. But as you savor this second helping of the Greatest Batman Stories Ever Told, bear in mind that there are many more yet to be created. And you will probably someday be able to read them, in future editions of this series—because in this, the third Year of The Bat in as many decades, one thing is certain: whether you know him as the Caped Crusader, Masked Manhunter, Darknight Detective or simply The Dark Knight, the Batman's power to excite seems greater than ever. Indeed, it seems eternal.

THE DEADLIEST DUO

Foreword by Mike Gold

O.K. Everybody knows The Joker's the top bad guy in the Batman pantheon—and it's hard to dispute the top banana status of The Penguin and Catwoman. So it was natural that these two evil-doers would be selected to follow The Joker in the spotlight (Klieg lights would be a better term) for the *Batman Returns* movie—which, in turn, inspired the focus of this book.

All of which is just fine by me, as The Penguin and Catwoman are my favorite blackguards, and they always were. But, for the life of me, I don't quite understand how they were able to achieve such a reaction. I figure I must have been born knowing about these scoundrels.

In doing the research needed to select these stories, Editors Bob Greenberger and Paul Kupperberg happened across an interesting revelation: there were hardly any Penguin or Catwoman stories published in the late 1950s and early 1960s. Actually, this was true of all of the big-name Batman villains: As I noted in the introduction to THE GREATEST JOKER STORIES EVER TOLD, when the Comics Code went into effect in the mid-1950s, DC decided to move away from the "traditional" villains into the realm of science-fiction inspired storylines. This also was in keeping with the motion picture trends of the time, where cheapo alien invasion stories brought them into the popcorn palaces in droves.

But I started reading Batman around 1957, and I was aware of The Penguin and Catwoman long before their stories were reprinted

in those phenomenal BATMAN ANNUALs of the early 1960s. So where did this knowledge come from?

I can only guess that I was inspired by tales of legend expressed by my older sister, herself a comic book reader, or perhaps by an older cousin who had been a Batman reader since the early 1940s. Clearly, The Penguin and Catwoman were extremely memorable characters, and I suspect their sagas were "handed down" to me the way stories had been handed down for centuries before Gutenberg.

All I know is, I became their fan long before I became their reader. Somebody successfully communicated the wonderment that creates these legends.

When Editor Julius Schwartz reintroduced The Batman in 1964, he started to bring back all of the classic villains, establishing a rogues gallery that rivaled the one he and his creative crew had established in THE FLASH. All of a sudden the Joker, the Penguin, Catwoman, Two-Face, the Mad Hatter, and Scarecrow were back on the scene.

This wasn't a stab in the dark—Julie's instincts, as usual, were right on the money. When the folks at 20th Century-Fox started up their

now-classic Batman television series less than two years later, they had a wealth of fantastic characters to exploit. Indeed, they led with The Riddler, a villain who had made but two appearances, both seventeen years prior to the launch of the television series. Although Frank Gorshin's entertaining and energetic performance in no way reminded older readers of Fred Astaire, the original inspiration for The Riddler's visual appearance, it was more than sufficient to burn the character into the viewers' minds and to establish the tone for the upcoming series.

It is no coincidence that the Penguin and Catwoman were among the most memorable television villains—not simply because the concept and the imagery of these characters was so significant, but because the actors who portrayed these villains were the cream of the crop. Burgess Meredith, one of America's most gifted and versatile performers, donned tuxedo, umbrella and body padding to transcend the limitations of the campy television series with his broad yet truly memorable creation. While the comic book Penguin was a formidable character, the post-television incarnation became a truly deadly adversary. Clearly the makeover was motivated, in part, by a desire to distance the Batman myth from the humorous atmosphere of the television series—yet the demand for the Penguin created by the show remained high for these ensuing two dozen years.

A penguin is a rather enigmatic animal: it is a bird, yet it does not fly; it swims, but is not a fish. Our Penguin is an extremely enigmatic villain: he dresses up in a tuxedo with tails, but he is no gentleman attending a dinner party. He is no gentleman at all.

Now, people dressed in tuxes often are referred to as wearing penguin suits, and as those of us who have seen *The Blues Brothers* know, it is not uncommon to refer to nuns as penguins as well. I am relieved to report that we have yet to come across an example of our Penguin being influenced by the latter reference.

He has been preoccupied with bird-themed crimes (and it's amazing that this narrow fixation did not impose undue limitations on his career), but his most enigmatic personality quirk is his fixation with umbrellas, a device not commonly associated with either fish or fowl. Of course, The Penguin's umbrellas tend to be cleverly-rigged instruments of death—or, in the case of the movie *Batman Returns*, a mode of transportation that compensates for this bird's inability to fly.

In other words, The Penguin is a pretty wacky guy—impressive because of his affectations more than his deeds, although in recent years his actions have grown much darker, consistent with the evolved mood of the contemporary Batman comics.

It has taken no less than three talented actors to create the part of Catwoman—Julie Newmar, the first to play the part on television, Lee Ann Meriwether, who played it solely in the 1966 theatrical motion picture, and Eartha Kitt, who imparted a strong, salacious quality to the character during the final season.

It was Kitt's downright sexiness that was most true to the evolution of Catwoman. In the aggregate, Catwoman has followed a rather twisted career path: a cat burglar who was The Batman's sworn enemy, it wasn't too long before she developed a romantic attraction to the Darknight Detective.

Such a desire certainly has its precedents in heroic fiction—the concept of the moody male hero sexually felling his female adversary is by no means unique. In the

case of Catwoman, however, her attentions seemed to go beyond the cliché—and even beyond the typical identification-with-the-aggressor syndrome similarly typical of popular fiction. Her love was genuine; there was something pure about her emotions towards The Batman.

The sexually aloof Batman always has remained rather beyond such base desires—generally speaking. But most remarkably, The Batman often has found himself succumbing (in one form or another) to Catwoman's charms. Quite frankly, he seemed to find Catwoman more…appealing…than alter ego Bruce Wayne ever found his "legitimate" girlfriends, Julie Madison and Vicki Vale. It was this dichotomy that makes the Batman/Catwoman relationship fascinating.

Her feelings towards The Batman had a ping-pong effect on her résumé. Starting out as a villain, she took on the heroic role in an effort to prove her worthiness to the object of her desire. When things didn't work out, Catwoman found herself drifting back to a life of crime—and flowing back to the other side of the stream as a reflec-

tion of her moral ambiguity.

In the process, Catwoman's travails clearly illustrates the schizophrenic role of the so-called superhero: as vigilantes, costumed heroes blatantly ignore the very legal structure they purport to hold dear. Even those heroes who have been "duly deputized by the police" are a civil libertarian's worst nightmare, as they are in constant violation of the fourth, fifth, sixth, seventh, and eighth amendments to the United States Constitution. Viewing it from this perspective, The Batman is a hypocrite, whereas Catwoman merely possesses a confused soul.

You may notice that, unlike the previous books in our GREATEST STORIES series, this volume largely concentrates on stories from the past three decades. As noted, there weren't very many Penguin or Catwoman stories in the years that preceded Editor Schwartz's takeover and, quite frankly, the quality of many of those few stories was rather… varied. Additionally, we already reprinted a number of the better early Penguin and Catwoman stories in our earlier GREATEST

STORIES books. (Oddly, THE GREATEST BATMAN STORIES EVER TOLD, VOLUME 2 is actually the third BATMAN volume, the aforementioned GREATEST JOKER STORIES book being the *real* volume two. If the time comes when the decision is made to do a sequel to the Joker book, perhaps we should move to lettering this series: THE GREATEST BATMAN STORIES VOLUME D, or somesuch.)

I should further point out that the early Penguin and Catwoman stories are being systematically reprinted in order as part of the complete reprinting of the DETECTIVE COMICS and BATMAN series, in our ongoing ARCHIVE EDITIONS. In the interest of historical perspective, however, we did not let the availability of these ARCHIVES books stop us from reprinting (*re-reprinting?*) the very first Penguin and Catwoman stories in this book.

Fans of our little menagerie of evildoers can find a nearly endless supply of books reprinting other classic sagas, in addition to the other books in our GREATEST STORIES and ARCHIVE EDITIONS series. Recently, Kitchen Sink and DC Comics teamed up to produce BATMAN: THE SUNDAY CLASSICS, reprinting several Penguin and Catwoman newspaper strip stories (in color, no less) from the mid-1940s. In the mid-1960s, Signet books issued a number of paperbacks reprinting classic stories, in black and white (with panels rearranged to fit the 4" by 6 3/4" format). One of these volumes was dedicated to Penguin stories, and this paperback series was re-reprinted in 1989 by Titan Books of England with the addition of a Catwoman collection.

Two of the most significant Catwoman sagas of the modern period remain in print in trade paperback form: the Frank Miller/David Mazzucchelli/Richmond Lewis BATMAN: YEAR ONE, and the Mindy Newell/J.J. Birch/Michael Bair/Adrienne Roy CATWOMAN: HER SISTER'S KEEPER. Both stories feature an updated —some might feel controversial— view of the classic villain.

Furthermore, Batman initiator Bob Kane's autobiography, *Batman & Me* (Eclipse Books, 1989) contains his views and recollections as to the creation of these and other pillars of the Batman community.

These days, there is no shortage of Penguin and Catwoman stories from all five decades of Batman history. Young readers need not rely on television reruns or genetic imprinting to experience firsthand the sense of wonder generated by the classic super-hero/super-villain confrontations.

To those of you who are looking at the following stories as revisiting old friends, welcome back. To those of you who are coming across these mini-epics for the first time, I envy you.

Here's where the fun *really* starts.

BRENT ANDERSON

(DC Comics' Group Editor/Director of Development Mike Gold is the editor of the other volumes in THE GREATEST STORIES EVER TOLD series, including the forthcoming multi-volume GREATEST 1960s STORIES EVER TOLD set, and is the former Consulting Editor of the ARCHIVE EDITIONS series.)

Written by Bill Finger/Art by Bob Kane & Jerry Robinson/Lettering by Jerry Robinson

READING ABOUT THE TRAVERS YACHT PARTY, EH? IT SURE IS GETTING A LOT OF PUBLICITY! EVERYONE KNOWS ABOUT IT!

THAT'S THE TROUBLE EVERY CROOK IN TOWN WILL BE THINKING ABOUT STEALING THAT NECKLACE IF HE CAN!

CALL IT A HUNCH! I'D LIKE TO BE ON THAT YACHT TOMORROW NIGHT, BUT I'VE ANOTHER JOB TO DO FIRST! I WONDER. HMMM....

DO YOU THINK THERE MIGHT BE TROUBLE? THAT SOMETHING MIGHT HAPPEN?

DICK, HOW WOULD YOU LIKE TO TAKE CHARGE OF THIS CASE UNTIL I GET THERE IN TIME TO HELP YOU? THINK YOU CAN DO IT ALONE?

ME? ALONE? AND HOW! LEAD ME TO IT!

BUT HOW WOULD I GET ON THE YACHT WITHOUT BEING SUSPECTED?

I KNOW A LOT OF PEOPLE. I'LL GET YOU A JOB AS A STEWARD THERE. FROM THEN ON YOU'RE ON YOUR OWN! NOW LISTEN CAREFULLY...

AND SO IT IS THAT YOUNG DICK GRAYSON IS ABOARD THE DOLPHIN...

BETTER KEEP MY EYES AND EARS OPEN. SAY, THERE'S MRS. TRAVERS... THINK I'LL EAVESDROP...

AH, DENNY, MY FAVORITE NEPHEW! WHERE HAVE YOU BEEN?

HELLO, AUNT MARTHA. I WANT YOU TO MEET MISS PEGGS. SHE IS A GUEST OF MINE! I HOPE YOU DON'T MIND MY BRINGING HER ABOARD?

2.

NONSENSE! GLAD TO HAVE MISS PEGGS!

THANK YOU! EVER SINCE I SPRAINED MY ANKLE DENNY HAS BEEN ESCORTING ME ABOUT! A FINE BOY, YOUR NEPHEW. A FINE BOY!

DICK "PUMPS" ONE OF THE REGULAR STEWARDS!

MUST BE A NICE FELLOW, HER NEPHEW, TO ESCORT AN OLD WOMAN AROUND LIKE THAT!

HUH, HIM? HE'S A RAT... PROBABLY HANGING AROUND TO GET SOME MONEY OUT OF HER! HE'S ALWAYS BORROWING DOUGH FROM HIS AUNT MRS. TRAVERS!

THEY ALL TRY TO GET DOUGH OUT OF HER! SEE THAT GUY WHO JUST WALKED OVER? THAT'S HER DOCTOR...WALLACE. GAMBLES ALL HIS DOUGH AWAY...AND THEN HE BORROWS MONEY FROM MRS. TRAVERS! I BET HE OWES HER PLENTY!... **PLENTY!**

SOMETIME LATER AS DICK PASSES A CABIN...

VOICES! SOUNDS LIKE A QUARREL!

NO! I WON'T LEND YOU A CENT, ROGER AND THAT'S **FINAL!**

BUT I NEED IT TO COVER MY STOCK LOSSES! PLEASE!

JUST BECAUSE YOU'RE MY BROTHER, DOESN'T MEAN I MUST FINANCE ALL YOUR STUPID PLUNGES IN THE STOCK MARKET!

I'LL BE RUINED! AND YOU'LL BE THE CAUSE OF IT ALL! I'LL GET THAT MONEY SOMEHOW SOMEWAY!

WHEW! LOOKS LIKE THIS YACHT ISN'T THE SAFEST PLACE IN THE WORLD FOR A NECKLACE WORTH A HALF A MILLION DOLLARS!

AS HE TURNS A CORNER HE SEES DENNY FURTIVELY THROW A PAPER OVER THE RAIL!

IF EVER A GUY LOOKED GUILTY ABOUT SOMETHING, HE DOES! WONDER WHAT'S IN THAT PAPER?

BY A QUEER QUIRK OF FATE, THE WIND SEIZES THE PAPER AND TOSSES IT BACK ON DECK...

WHAT A BREAK! NOW TO READ IT!

THE GUNMEN ARE DISARMED!

HOW DID YOU GET HERE?

THE TRAIL GOT COLD ON MY OTHER CASE, SO I DROVE TO THE YACHT! WHEN I SAW THIS LAUNCH SPEEDING AWAY, I FIGURED SOMETHING WAS UP. SO HERE I AM!

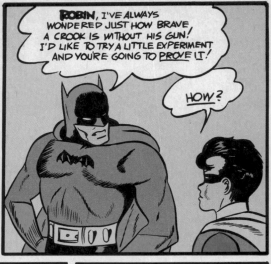

ROBIN, I'VE ALWAYS WONDERED JUST HOW BRAVE A CROOK IS WITHOUT HIS GUN! I'D LIKE TO TRY A LITTLE EXPERIMENT AND YOU'RE GOING TO PROVE IT!

HOW?

I'M GOING TO SHOW THE KIDS OF AMERICA HOW YELLOW YOU RATS ARE WITHOUT YOUR GUNS! I'M GOING TO LET **ROBIN** HERE TAKE FOUR OF YOU ON ALL AT THE SAME TIME!

THE GUY'S NUTS!

FOUR OF US AGAINST THAT KID! HA-HA-HA!

THAT'S MY PROPOSITION. TAKE IT?

AND HOW! JUST LET ME GET MY HANDS ON HIM!

A MOMENT LATER· A STARTLING SCENE TAKES PLACE· FOUR GROWN MEN PIT THEIR STRENGTH AGAINST THAT OF A LONE BOY!!

WE'LL KNOCK THE KID SILLY!

I'M AFRAID YOU'RE THE ONES WHO ARE GOING TO FEEL SILLY!

ROBIN ACTS WITH THE SPEED OF THOUGHT!

FANCY BUMPING INTO YOU BOYS·· WAY OUT HERE!

③

THEN A FIST THAT SHOOTS OUT WITH THE FORCE OF A PISTON-ROD!

COME, COME, BOYS, HOW ABOUT A LITTLE COMPETITION!

AS THE PANIC-STRICKEN PEOPLE DASH OUT··THE BATMAN NOTICES A STRANGE THING···MISS PEGGS IS RUNNING LIKE A MUCH YOUNGER PERSON··AND WITHOUT A LIMP!!

IT WORKED!··THERE GOES MISS PEGGS··NICE LEGS FOR AN OLD WOMAN!

THE CAPTAIN APPEARS AND SHOUTS OUT WORDS THAT ALMOST HYPNOTIZE THE PEOPLE TO ORDER···

STOP!··THERE'S NO FIRE!··IT'S A FALSE ALARM!SOME CRAZY FOOL MUST HAVE SET THE ALARM OFF AS A JOKE!!!

A FALSE ALARM···I WONDER···THE BATMAN···HE'S AFTER ME!!··IT'S A TRAP!

BUT EVEN AS SHE DESCENDS THE STAIRS··A FIGURE HURTLES AFTER HER!

ROBIN··THE BOY WONDER·· COMES THROUGH AGAIN!!

MY MOTHER TOLD ME NEVER TO FIGHT WITH A LADY··BUT THIS TIME I'M MAKING AN EXCEPTION!!

THE BATMAN TAKES CHARGE!

···NOW I'M GOING TO SHOW YOU WHAT THE REAL CAT LOOKS LIKE!·· I'VE HEARD TALES ABOUT THE CAT BEFORE IN THE UNDERWORLD!

I CAN HARDLY WAIT!

BLACK HAIR IS REVEALED UNDER THE GREY WIG!

FIRST··OFF WITH THE WIG!

YOU··· YOU···!!

BOY, HE'S OUT COLDER THAN A DEAD MACKEREL!

BATMAN... I WAS SUPPOSED TO GIVE DENNY HALF OF THE JEWELS... WHY DON'T YOU COME IN AS A PARTNER WITH ME! YOU AND I TOGETHER!

YOU AND I KING AND QUEEN OF CRIME!... WE'D MAKE A GREAT TEAM! WITH YOU AS MY PARTNER WE...

SORRY, YOUR PROPOSITION TEMPTS ME BUT WE WORK ON DIFFERENT SIDES OF THE LAW! LET'S GO!

"WITH THE JEWELS GIVEN TO MRS. TRAVERS...AND HER NEPHEW LOCKED IN HIS CABIN...THE BATMAN AND ROBIN ARE HOME-WARD BOUND...WITH THE CAT!"

WELL, WE'RE HOME. THERE'S THE WHARF NOW!

WHY DIDN'T YOU LEAVE ME BEHIND ON THE YACHT INSTEAD OF TAKING ME TO THE POLICE YOURSELF?

I'VE GOT MY REASONS!

"SUDDENLY THE CAT LEAPS TO HER FEET AND..."

WATCH HER...SHE'S JUMPED OVERBOARD!

FANCY THAT.

"AS ROBIN MAKES READY TO JUMP AFTER THE CAT...THE BATMAN CLUMSILY 'BUMPS' INTO HIM!"

HEY!

OOPS-SORRY, ROBIN!

"BY THE TIME THEY RECOVER, THE CAT HAS MADE GOOD HER ESCAPE!"

TOO LATE...SHE'S GONE!...AND...SAY...I'LL BET YOU BUMPED INTO ME ON PURPOSE! THAT'S WHY YOU TOOK HER ALONG WITH US...SO SHE MIGHT TRY A BREAK!

WHY, ROBIN, MY BOY, WHATEVER GAVE YOU SUCH AN IDEA!... HMM...NICE NIGHT, ISN'T IT?

...LOVELY GIRL!...WHAT EYES!... SAY...MUSTN'T FORGET I'VE GOT A GIRL NAMED JULIE!... OH WELL...SHE STILL HAD LOVELY EYES!...MAYBE I'LL BUMP INTO HER AGAIN SOMETIME...

HMMM...

BOB KANE

(13)

"SO MANY OF OUR READERS HAVE WRITTEN US SUCH NICE LETTERS THAT WE HAVE DECIDED TO SHOW OUR APPRECIATION.... THEREFORE ON THE BACK COVER OF THIS MAGAZINE YOU WILL FIND A FULL-PAGE AUTOGRAPHED PICTURE SUITABLE FOR FRAMING, OF BOTH BATMAN AND ROBIN THE BOY WONDER....

THIS IS OUR WAY OF SAYING THANKS....

Bob Kane

DICK LEARNS THAT ART CAN BE EXPENSIVE.

YES, DICK, THESE TWO SMALL WATTEAUS ARE WORTH ROUGHLY A HALF MILLION DOLLARS BETWEEN THEM!

WHEW! MAYBE I OUGHT TO TAKE UP PAINTING!

BEAUTIFUL--MARVELOUS--GORGEOUS--

LET'S GO BACK. YOU REALLY MUST LEARN NOT TO LAUGH AT PEOPLE OR THINGS, BECAUSE THEY MAY BE---ER-ODD LOOKING!

BUT, BRUCE, LOOK FOR YOURSELF!

HA! HA! HE DOES LOOK LIKE A PENGUIN AT THAT!

SUDDENLY!

NOBODY CAN LEAVE! THE TWO WATTEAU PAINTINGS HAVE BEEN CUT FROM THEIR FRAMES AND STOLEN--WE WILL HAVE TO SEARCH EVERYONE HERE!

THOSE ARE THE VERY PAINTINGS WE JUST WERE ADMIRING!

GOSH!

RICH MAN--POOR MAN--BEGGARMAN--AND THIEF--ALL MUST SUBMIT TO THE SEARCH!

I'M AFRAID THIS IS GOING TO BE--ER--EMBARRASSING!

I DON'T MIND A-BEIN' SEARCH! I ONLY HOPE -A DEY CATCH DA THIEF!

IT'S OUTRAGEOUS! IMAGINE SEARCHING ME!

CURSES! THERE GOES A MILLION DOLLARS!

COUNT PEREL! WHY, YOU'RE NOTHING BUT A PHONEY! GOODBYE!

LOOKS LIKE FINE FEATHERS DON'T ALWAYS MAKE FINE BIRDS!

BRUCE AND DICK SUBMIT UNCOMPLAININOLY TO BEING SEARCHED!

SORRY, MR. WAYNE, BUT WE GOTTA CHECK EVERYBODY!

PERFECTLY ALL RIGHT, JONES!

I'D TAKE OFF MY SHOES, BUT I'VE GOT A HOLE IN MY STOCKING.

THE GUARDS ARE BAFFLED AS THEIR SEARCH ENDS FRUITLESSLY!

SORRY TO DISAPPOINT YOU- HEE--HEE--- DON'T YOU KNOW IT'S BAD LUCK TO OPEN AN UMBRELLA INDOORS?

HE AIN'T GOT THEM EITHER. THEY WOULDN'T HAVE FLOWN AWAY!

THAT NIGHT, IN A HOTEL OF THE BIGGEST RACKETEERS IN TOWN-- KNOWN SIMPLY AS THE BOSS-- A FAT FIGURE WADDLES IN!

PARDON ME-- BUT AREN'T YOU THE GENTLEMAN WHO CONTROLS ALL THE RACKETEERING IN THIS TOWN?

SAY-- YOU'VE GOT THE NERVE!

WHAT DO YOU WANT?

DID YOU HEAR OF THE HALF MILLION DOLLARS' WORTH OF PAINTINGS THAT WERE---ER... STOLEN FROM THE ART EXHIBITION?

SHALL I DRILL HIM, BOSS?

WAIT A MINUTE-- LET'S HEAR HIS SPIEL!

HOLY SMOKE! BROTHER, YOU'RE IN-- SAY, WHAT'S YOUR HANDLE?

OH--AH--I HAVE SO MANY! WHY NOT CALL ME THE PENGUIN? IT DOES FIT-- HEE-- HEE!

BEFORE LONG, THE PENGUIN DIRECTS THE ACTIVITIES OF THE BOSS' MOB!

THE WAY WE'LL PULL OUR JOB IS BY GOING THROUGH THIS ABANDONED GAS PIPE--AND COMING UP UNDER THE BANK HERE!

YOU TELL 'EM, PENGUIN!

NEWSPAPER HEADLINES CALL FOR ACTION AS A CRIME-WAVE THREATENS TO ENGULF THE CITY?

ORGANIZED CRIME THREATENS THE CITY

SUN

HAND OF CRIME MASTER SEEN BACK OF SERIES OF ROBBERIES

NEXT DAY---AT THE STAHL AUCTIONEERING HOUSE---

IF I'M NOT MISTAKEN, THAT'S THE FATTY DICK AND I SAW AT THE EXHIBITION. THAT UMBRELLA-- MUST BE ATTACHED TO HIM!

EXCUSE ME--

THIS COLUMBIA DIAMOND IS THE FINEST WHITE STONE IN THE WORLD...

SUDDENLY--THE ROOM PLUNGES INTO DARKNESS--

SOCK!

BAM!

WHEN THE LIGHTS ARE TURNED ON?

THE DIAMOND... THE GREAT COLUMBIA DIAMOND... IT'S GONE!

FRENZIED VOICES FILL THE AIR AND PEOPLE MILL ABOUT EXCITEDLY--

SORRY-- I WAS SO EXCITED WHEN THE LIGHTS WENT OUT--I DIDN'T KNOW WHAT I WAS DOING!

WHAT'S THE IDEA-- TRIPPING ME?

SO SORRY YOU WERE INCONVENIENCED!

QUITE ALL RIGHT! ER--- NO HARM DONE!

I'VE GOT A HUNCH THAT KEEPS GROWING. EACH TIME I BUMP INTO THAT LITTLE GUY, SOMETHING HAPPENS-- I THINK I'LL GO SLUMMING TONIGHT.

LATER--AT THE BOSS' HEADQUARTERS--

I INSIST ON MY USUAL SHARE OF MONEY FOR ROBBERIES I'VE PLANNED!

YOU'RE GETTIN' TOO BIG FOR YOUR SHOES-- I'VE GOTTA TEACH YA A LESSON SO'S YOU WON'T STEP INTO MINE!

AAAAGH!

THIS WAS BOUND TO OCCUR SOONER OR LATER--- MIGHT AS WELL GET IT OVER WITH NOW!

BANG!

IF NONE OF YOU LADS OBJECTS--I'M YOUR NEW BOSS!

SURE-- IT'S OKAY WITH ME, MR. PENGUIN!

SURE!

THAT NIGHT, THE PENGUIN'S HENCHMEN DISCUSS PLANS IN A WATERFRONT DIVE!

DAT JOB DE PENGUIN PLANNED FER TONIGHT WILL BE A CINCH-- ALL WE GOTTA DO IS HEIST A LITTLE JADE IDOL FROM DE VAULT OF DAT STAHL AUCTIONEERIN' HOUSE!

PIPE DOWN, YA DOPE! SOMEBODY MIGHT BE LISTENING!

4

REMOVAL OF PUTTY AND A WIG REVEAL THE CLEAN CUT FEATURES OF BRUCE WAYNE--

HOW'D YOU MAKE OUT?

I FOUND OUT PLENTY-- AND YOU CAN'T GO WITH ME—YOU'VE GOT HOMEWORK TO DO!

THAT NIGHT--- THE BATMAN CLIMBS TO THE ROOF OF THE STAHL AUCTIONEERING HOUSE---

INSIDE THE TOP-FLOOR OFFICE OF THE STAHL AUCTIONEERS-- A SEARING FLAME PLAYS UPON THE METAL OF A GREAT, OLD-FASHIONED VAULT!

UNMINDFUL OF THE ODDS AGAINST HIM--THE BATMAN HURTLES TOWARDS THE THUGS BELOW!

IT'S THE BATMAN!

THANKS FOR WAVING AT ME, BOYS! IT'S A BIT HOT IN HERE!

OOF!

UGH!

BATMAN BENDS LOW AS THE DEADLY FLAME FROM THE ACETYLENE TORCH SHOOTS OVER HIS HEAD!

A WARM RECEPTION BATMAN? HAW!

AND YOU'RE NOT FOOLING, CHUM!

SNATCHING THE OIL PAINTING FROM THE WALL, THE BATMAN WHIPS ABOUT--

EVER GO IN FOR ART? YOU MAY FIND THIS A STRIKING EXAMPLE!

HA--HA-- A PICTURE NO ARTIST COULD DO JUSTICE TO. WELL, I COULD STAND AND ADMIRE YOU FOREVER, BUT---

--BUSINESS BEFORE PLEASURE!

OW!

UGH!

5

STILL DAZED, THE BATMAN IS TAKEN TO A 'LUXURIOUS' MANSION--

WHERE AM I?-- WHY DID YOU BRING ME HERE?

JUST FORMALITY, BATMAN! WE WANT YOU TO TELL MR. BONIFACE WHAT HAPPENED TO HIS IDOL--

A PUDGY FIGURE TODDLES IN-- THE PENGUIN!

THAT'S HIM! I'D RECOGNIZE THAT MASK AND CLOAK OF HIS ANYWHERE--

AM I GOING CRAZY? HE'S--

BUT, MR. BONIFACE, YOU MUST BE WRONG! THIS IS THE BATMAN!

I DON'T CARE! HE'S BEEN THREATENING ME FOR WEEKS! HE SAID I'D HAVE TO PAY HIM FOR PROTECTION-- AND THAT HE STOOD IN SO WELL WITH THE POLICE, THAT NOBODY WOULD BELIEVE ME IF I COMPLAINED! I WANT HIM LOCKED UP!

DON'T WORRY, SIR--WE'LL TAKE CARE OF HIM!

THANK YOU-- I WAS SURE YOU'D SEE YOUR DUTY!

THAT GAS-- I CAN'T THINK--

AS THE POLICE VAN--CONTAINING THE BATMAN--GOES DOWN THE STREET, A SLEEK BLACK CAR MOVES FROM ITS POSITION ON THE CORNER!

NOW WE FINISH THE REST OF THE PENGUIN'S PLANS!

SUDDENLY-- THE BLACK CAR DELIBERATELY SIDESWIPES THE POLICE VAN--

CRASH!

7

GRAB 'IM! THE PENGUIN WANTS 'IM!

AS THE UNCONSCIOUS POLICE SPRAWL IN THE GUTTER, THE THUGS POUNCE UPON THE DAZED BATMAN--

LATER--IN THE PENGUIN'S MANSION---

WHY DID YOU BRING ME HERE AFTER CONVINCING THE POLICE THAT I'M A CROOK?

FOR SEVERAL REASONS, MY DEAR BATMAN-- FIRST I COLLECT INSURANCE ON MY OWN LITTLE PIECE OF JADE--

SECONDLY--I REMAIN IN THE CLEAR AS AN INNOCENT COLLECTOR! I KNEW THAT WE WOULD INEVITABLY COME TO GRIPS--SO--I MADE PLANS. I'VE CALLED THE POLICE AND THERE'S AN ALARM OUT FOR YOU!

THE BLARING RADIO EXPLAINS--

CALLING ALL CARS--- PICK UP BATMAN- ROBBED STAHL AUCTIONEERS-- ESCAPED AS HE WAS BEING BROUGHT TO JAIL!

YOU SEE?

I SEE? A FRAME- UP! IF I STAY HERE, I'M GUILTY --AND IF I ESCAPE, I'LL GET SHOT BY THE POLICE!

THE SITUATION SEEMS HOPELESS--WHEN A DARING THOUGHT STRIKES THE BATMAN-

ONLY A SMALL CHANCE-- BUT IT'S A CHANCE IF DICK IS AT HOME!

LET'S NOT DWELL UPON SUCH UNPLEASANT THOUGHTS. LET US ADMIRE MY UMBRELLAS-- HMM-- HMM!

THE BATMAN'S FEET COME TOGETHER IN AN APPARENTLY INNOCENT MOVEMENT

WATCHA DOING?

MY FOOT ITCHES--AND IF YOU WON'T UNTIE MY HANDS I'LL SIMPLY HAVE TO SCRATCH WITH MY FEET!

HMMM! GOT THIS ONE IN SPAIN! HMM!

THE PRESSURE OF A FOOT AND THE SWITCH OF THE TWO-WAY TELEPHONE CONCEALED IN THE BATMAN'S FOOT CLICKS!

BATMAN'S FOOT BEGINS TAPPING ON THE FLOOR IN A STRANGE MANNER--

MIGHT AS WELL CATCH UP WITH MY DANCING--- SITTING DOWN!

AT THE HOME OF BRUCE WAYNE, DICK GRAYSON HAS HEARD THE POLICE RADIO CALLS DENOUNCING THE BATMAN- DICK GOES INTO ACTION AS ROBIN THE BOY WONDER-

THEY CAN'T CALL BATMAN A MURDERER! I'LL FIND HIM SOME- HOW, AND--SAY-- MY TELEPHONE BELT--IT'S TAPPING A MESSAGE--IN MORSE CODE...

ROBIN.. I'M BEING HELD IN THE MANSION ON THE CORNER OF LINCOLN AVENUE.. HURRY----

THE RESOURCEFUL BATMAN TAPS HIS FOOT IN MORSE CODE INFORMING ROBIN OF HIS WHEREABOUTS!

AND ANOTHER PERSON IS ALSO WORRIED--AND BROKEN--- COMMISSIONER GORDON--

THE BATMAN-- TURNED CRIMINAL-- I CAN'T BELIEVE IT! WHY DID HE DO IT--WHY?

SOON AFTER---THE PENGUIN'S HOUSE ON THE CORNER OF LINCOLN AVENUE---

WHO RANG THE BELL?

IT'S A TELEGRAM MESSENGER!

AND HERE'S YOUR MESSAGE!

SSSPPLLFF!

ROBIN DASHES INSIDE THE HOUSE--BUT FINDS THE ODDS AGAINST HIM ARE MANY---

STOP THIS KID--HE WORKS WITH THE BATMAN!

I'LL STOP HIM-- FER GOOD!

GOSH! I'M GETTING POPULAR-- ER--NICE HEADWORK, BOYS!

OUCH!

GOT YOU-- OOOUH!

AS IF RELEASED BY A GIANT SPRING--ROBIN'S AGILE BODY CRASHES AGAINST THE HEAVILY LADEN TABLE---

GOT IT! NICE WORK, ROBIN!

OOOPS! HOW CLUMSY OF ME-- DON'T CUT YOURSELF, BATMAN- GOT IT!

AS ROBIN WHIRLS TO MEET THE CHARGING THUGS--BATMAN HURLS HIS BOUND BODY--AND THE CHAIR TO WHICH HE IS ATTACHED--TO THE FLOOR-

I'VE GOT TO CUT THESE CORDS-- AND QUICKLY!

JAGGED BITS OF BROKEN GLASS SEVER THE BATMAN'S BONDS---AS ROBIN BRAVELY TACKLES BOTH THUGS--

ULP!

GOTTA CUT THIS KID DOWN BEFORE THE **BATMAN** FREES HIMSELF!

MUST HURRY--AH! THE STRANDS ARE PARTING!

THE BATMAN, FREED, LEAPS AT THE STRUGGLING GROUP IN TIME--

OHHH!

HOLD 'IM WHILE I KNOCK OUT HIS TEETH!

BETTER COUNT YOUR OWN TEETH--

--BECAUSE YOU WON'T HAVE THEM FOR LONG!

BUT VICTORY TURNS TO DEFEAT AS THE OILY VOICE OF THE PENGUIN CUTS THRU THE SOUNDS OF BATTLE.

ALL RIGHT, GENTLEMEN-- PLEASE STAND AT EASE!

TAKE IT EASY, ROBIN-- HIS UMBRELLAS ARE MORE DANGEROUS THAN GUNS!

THE PENGUIN'S HAND REACHES FOR HIS PHONE--

HMM ---GLAD TO SEE YOU ACTING SENSIBLE, BATMAN--UH-- HELLO, OPERATOR, GIVE ME THE POLICE!-- THIS IS MR. BONIFACE-- I'VE GOT THE BATMAN AT MY HOME --- NO, DON'T THANK ME--

C'MON, ROBIN-- THIS IS ONE TIME STRATEGIC RETREAT IS SMARTER THAN COMPLETE DEFEAT! LET'S GO!

I'M RIGHT BEHIND YOU!

THEY'RE GETTIN' AWAY!

STOP THEM!

POLICE RUSHING IN, FIND THAT BATMAN HAS ESCAPED!

WHERE'S THE BATMAN? YOU SAID YOU HAD HIM HERE!

SO I DID, BUT HE--AH--LEFT RATHER ABRUPTLY!

BATMAN AND ROBIN SPEED TO THEIR APARTMENT--

OUR BIRD-LIKE FRIEND SHOULD BE ABOUT READY FOR A SUPER-COUP. THE POLICE ARE AFTER ME-- AND HE IS IN THE CLEAR! I THINK THE TRAIL IS WINDING TO AN END --ONE WAY OR ANOTHER!

NIGHT AFTER NIGHT, A BLIND MAN IS SEEN STANDING NEAR THE PENGUIN'S MANSION, HIS QUAVERING VOICE CALLING FOR ALMS. THEN, ONE DARK NIGHT--

THIS JOB'LL BE EASY-- WE GOT ALL THE GROUNDWORK LAID OUT!

IN THE HEART OF THE BOWERY... WHERE HUMBLE FLOP-HOUSES RUB SHOULDERS WITH TALL, STATELY BUILDINGS THAT HOUSE UNTOLD WEALTH, HERE IS WHERE THE GREAT DIAMOND EXCHANGES MAKE THEIR OFFICES!

GREETINGS, WE ARE HERE TO GET MORE INFORMATION FOR OUR LECTURES ON HUMAN PSYCHOLOGY. ARE OUR--ER--CHAMBERS INTACT?

I NEVER RENT IT TO NOBODY BUT YOU-- JUST LIKE YOU ORDERED!

IN THE PENGUIN'S ROOM---

THAT CLERK WOULD CERTAINLY BE LESS POLITE IF HE KNEW THAT WE ARE TUNNELIN' THRU THE WALL INTO THE DIAMOND EXCHANGE!

HURRY, MEN! WE'LL HAVE TO USE THE ACETYLENE TORCH ON THE STEEL SIDES OF THE VAULT--

MEANWHILE IN THE STREET---

THERE THEY ARE- I RECOGNIZE THEIR SHADOWS!

FOR A BLIND MAN---YOU SEE PRETTY GOOD!

MINUTES PASS AS THE ODD PAIR KEEPS THEIR CEASELESS VIGIL-- AND THEN---

JUST AS I SUSPECTED--THEY'VE TUNNELED THROUGH THEIR ROOM AND INTO THE DIAMOND EXCHANGE BUILDING! LET'S GO!

DIAMOND EXCHANGE

In the darkened alleyway, the blind man and the urchin rip off their outer clothes, and are revealed as the Batman and Robin—

We'll have to work fast, Robin!

Here I come!

The Batman and Robin move upward until they reach the level of the lighted window!

Charming bits of glass. Their sparkles spell our fortunes!

We won't have time to open the window--or they'll spot us!

It's the Batman!

--And we spell misfortune!

This is for framing my pal!

And this thrown in for interest!

As the battle rages-the Penguin levels his deadly umbrella!

Amuse yourself, fools, for soon you--

Acid sprays from the stem of the umbrella---

DIE!

DOWN, ROBIN!

It's the Batman--and Mr. Penguin!

Outside--- policemen, attracted by the lighted window in the closed building, investigate-

Taking advantage of the momentary confusion-the Penguin makes a break for freedom---

You'll never get me, and I've still got the jewels! Hee! Hee!

12

RACING TO THE STREET BELOW-- THE PENGUIN CLATTERS UP THE STAIRS OF THE ELEVATED STATION.

WE'VE GOT HIM CORNERED, BATMAN!

WHAT'S YOUR HURRY? THERE'S STILL SOME UNFINISHED BUSINESS!

I'LL CROSS THE TRACKS AND--- UGH!

THE PENGUIN DROPS HIS UMBRELLA AS THE BATMAN'S FIST THUNDERS AGAINST HIS JAW!

GATHERING HIS STRENGTH IN ONE LAST EFFORT, THE PENGUIN WRESTLES BATMAN TO THE TRACKS--AS A TRAIN ROARS INTO THE STATION---

BATMAN! LOOK OUT! A TRAIN'S COMING!

AS THE METAL MONSTER ROARS DOWN UPON THE WRESTLING COMBATANTS-- AN UPTOWN EXPRESS THUNDERS TOWARDS THEM FROM THE OPPOSITE DIRECTION---

TEARING HIMSELF LOOSE FROM THE BATMAN'S GRIP--THE PENGUIN LEAPS FOR THE PASSING EXPRESS TRAIN

NOBODY CAN CATCH THE PENGUIN! HEE-HEE!

--AND THE OTHER STRING OF CARS PASS OVER THE BATMAN'S BODY!

AS THE LOCAL PULLS OUT OF THE STATION--

BATMAN! GOLLY--- B-BUT I WAS WORRIED!

I JUST LAY FLAT, ROBIN, AND THE CARS PASSED OVER ME--ER-- I WILL ADMIT, THOUGH, THAT I DIDN'T EXACTLY ENJOY THE SENSATION!

LATER, IN COMMISSIONER GORDON'S OFFICE--

ER---COUGH--- WE'RE SORRY WE SUSPECTED YOU, BATMAN, BUT OF COURSE I FELT ALL THE TIME THAT YOU WERE INNOCENT!

I KNOW THAT, GORDON, BUT THE MOST IMPORTANT THING IS THAT WE MISSED UP ON THE PENGUIN--YET SOMEHOW I FEEL WE'LL MEET HIM AGAIN!

YES---PERHAPS SOME DAY THE PATHS OF THE BATMAN AND THE _____ WILL CROSS AGAIN--

-THE END-

SOMEWHERE ON THE OUTSKIRTS OF GOTHAM CITY, AS HARD-FACED MEN LOOK EXPECTANTLY AT A MASKED FIGURE...

HA-HA.. ANOTHER HEADLINE ABOUT US! SO FAR WE'RE DOING FINE, BOYS .. BUT FOR THE OTHER ROBBERIES I'VE PLANNED, I'M GOING TO NEED A *PARTNER!*

GOT ANYBODY IN MIND, *MISTER X?*

GOTHAM NEWS

MR. X MOB ROBS CITY BANK!

NEW GANG CZAR'S THIRD HAUL THIS WEEK

YES-- THE CLEVEREST, MOST DANGEROUS-- AND MOST BEAUTIFUL LADY OF CRIME IN THE COUNTRY-- *THE CATWOMAN!*

CATWOMAN? BUT SHE'S IN JAIL!

THEN WE'LL GET HER OUT! YES, I KNOW JUST HOW TO DO IT...AND ONCE *CATWOMAN* IS FREE, NOTHING WILL STOP US! WE'LL EMBARK ON A CRIME WAVE THE LIKES OF WHICH GOTHAM CITY HAS NEVER BEFORE SEEN.'

SLAM!

NEXT DAY, IN THE HOME OF POLICE COMMISSIONER GORDON...

GOOD GRIEF, *BATMAN!* LOOK AT THAT HEAD-LINE ON THE TELE-VISION SCREEN! *CATWOMAN'S* OUT TO COMMIT MORE CRIMES!

CATWOMAN ESCAPES THROUGH DYNAMITED PRISON WALL!

NOT IF WE CAN HELP IT... RIGHT, *ROBIN?*

RIGHT, *BATMAN!*

WHILE ELSEWHERE, IN A SPEEDING CAR--THAT *PRINCESS OF PLUNDER--THE CATWOMAN.'*

SO YOUR *BOSS* PLANNED MY JAIL-BREAK, EH? BUT WHY?

HE NEEDS YOU FOR A DEAL, *CATWOMAN!* NOW I GOTTA *BLINDFOLD* YOU! *MISTER X'S* PLACE HAS TO BE KEPT SECRET--EVEN FROM YOU!

SOON, *CRIME QUEEN* MEETS *CRIME KING!*

MISTER X, I PRESUME.

CORRECT, *CATWOMAN...* LET'S GET DOWN TO BUSI-NESS! I'VE GOT MANY JOBS LINED UP FOR MY MOB. BUT IN ORDER TO WORK THEM, THE BOYS MIGHT HAVE TO KILL GUARDS OR WATCHMEN! THAT, I DON'T WANT... I DON'T EVER WANT A MURDER RAP HANGING OVER MY HEAD!

CATWOMAN, YOU ALWAYS ROB *WITHOUT KILLING*, BY USING YOUR KNOWLEDGE OF CATS! SO HERE'S MY OFFER -- *YOU DO THE JOBS FOR ME*, AND WE'LL SHARE THE LOOT! IF YOU REFUSE, I'LL DO THE JOBS ANYWAY! WHAT DO YOU SAY?

OKAY--WE'RE PARTNERS!

GOOD! *DIPPER*, HERE, WILL TELL YOU OF THE FIRST PLACE TO BE ROBBED! BY THE TIME WE'RE THROUGH, WE'LL HAVE COMMISSIONER GORDON GOING AROUND IN CIRCLES!

LATER, AS THE *CATWOMAN* AND DIPPER DISCUSS ROBBERY PLANS IN A CRIMINAL HANGOUT...

HYA, DIPPER OL' PAL! DID-DIDJA TALK TO *MISTER X* ABOUT ME JOINING HIS MOB, HUH?

BEAT IT, MOUSEY! *MISTER X* DON'T WANT YOU AROUND! HE LIKES GUYS WITH NERVE! IF THE COPS EVER *LOOKED* AT YOU, YOU'D FAINT!

AW, PLEASE, DIPPER. I'LL DO ANYTHING TO JOIN THE MOB! UGH! DON'T SHOVE!

HE'S ALWAYS AROUND, *CATWOMAN!* A REGULAR PEST! HE'S JUST LIKE HIS NAME-- *MOUSEY!*

CAREFUL MOUSEY, OR I'LL SEND THIS CAT AFTER YOU! HA-HA!

SPLAT

MEOWRR-

LATER, IN THE *CAT-WOMAN'S* EERIE LAIR...

YAWN I HATE TO LEAVE THIS WARM FIRE AND MY PRETTY PETS-- BUT IT'S TIME I LOOKED OVER THE FIRST PLACE I'M TO ROB! *YAWN*

MEOWRRR

PURR

PURR-RR

BUT AS SHE STEPS OUT INTO THE NIGHT...

YOUR HUNCH WAS RIGHT, *BATMAN!* HER HIDEOUT *IS* SOMEWHERE AROUND HERE! LET'S GO!

LOOK, *ROBIN!* IT'S THE *CATWOMAN!*

STEALTHILY, THE MASKED CRIME-BUSTERS CLOSE IN -- BUT SUDDENLY...

AH... I'VE BEEN EXPECTING YOU! MEET MY *RED PERSIAN* ...A CAT NOTED FOR A FIERY TEMPER THAT MATCHES ITS COLOR! BEING COOPED UP HAS MADE IT VERY IRRITATED! HA-HA!

ROBIN! WATCH OUT!

WHILE *ROBIN* PARRIES THE CLAWING CAT, *BATMAN* PURSUES THE FELINE FELON PAST A CONDEMNED BUILDING, WHERE...

OHH! A SECTION OF THE WALL IS TOPPLING! *BATMAN WILL BE KILLED!* I'LL BE ABLE TO ESCAPE NOW! I'LL BE FREE!

WARNING BE WARE OF FALLING BRICKS

BUT WAIT! FOR A SPLIT INSTANT, THE *CATWOMAN* HESITATES, THEN, LIKE A STREAK OF SABLE LIGHTNING, SHE LEAPS TO *SAVE BATMAN!*

GET BACK! BA... UHH!

WHAT..?

S-RASH

MOMENTS LATER... I SAW THAT, *BATMAN!* SHE RISKED HER LIFE TO SAVE YOU! I DON'T UNDERSTAND IT...SOMETIMES SHE ACTS LIKE THE *EXACT OPPOSITE!*

SHE'S STILL UNCONSCIOUS! WE'D BETTER RACE HER TO THE *BAT-CAVE*...SHE NEEDS EMERGENCY TREATMENT-- FAST!

PRESENTLY, IN THEIR SECRET *BAT-CAVE*...

SHE'S COMING TO!

LISTEN! WHAT'S SHE SAYING?

FASTEN YOUR SAFETY BELTS! IF WE REMAIN CALM THE PILOT WILL GET US DOWN *SAFELY!* FASTEN YOUR SAFETY BELTS!

THEN, AS HER EYES SNAP OPEN...

WH-WHERE AM I? WHERE ARE THE PASSENGERS? DID WE LAND SAFELY? WH-WHO ARE YOU?

CATWOMAN, YOU KNOW PERFECTLY WELL THAT WE'RE *BATMAN* AND *ROBIN!*

LATER, WHEN SELINA KYLE EXPLAINS THE FACTS TO THE COMMISSIONER...

CATWOMAN... ER... I MEAN MISS KYLE, IF YOU WISH TO ATONE FOR YOUR PAST CRIMES, YOU CAN DO SO BY BECOMING OUR UNDERCOVER AGENT!

THAT'S RIGHT, SELINA... YOU'RE OUR BEST LEAD TO MISTER X, SO WE WANT YOU TO REMAIN AS HIS PARTNER!

NO... PLEASE! I WANT TO PUT MY CRIMINAL PAST BEHIND ME!

YOU WILL... BUT AFTERWARD! REMEMBER, IF YOU PRETEND TO BE MISTER X'S PARTNER, THERE'LL BE NO MORE KILLINGS! YOU'LL BE DOING A PUBLIC SERVICE! AND IF MY PLAN WORKS, YOU'LL ONLY HAVE TO DO ONE JOB!

WITH YOU AS OUR SECRET OPERATIVE, WE'LL GET MISTER X, AND... WHA..?

COMMISSIONER, I JUST PICKED UP THIS PUNK FOR CARRYING A GUN! HE... ULP! SORRY, SIR... I THOUGHT YOU WERE ALONE!

MOUSEY!

THIS MAN IS DANGEROUS! HE'S ALWAYS WANTED TO JOIN MR. X'S GANG! NOW, HE'LL SURELY TELL MR. X ABOUT ME -- AS A BRIBE!

IN THAT CASE, WE MUST LOCK HIM UP! OFFICER, CHARGE HIM WITH CARRYING A CONCEALED WEAPON... NOBODY'S TO SEE HIM TILL THIS CASE IS FINISHED!

HUH? I'LL GET YOU FOR THIS, CATWOMAN!

AFTER MOUSEY IS LED OFF...

WELL, SELINA KYLE... ALIAS THE CATWOMAN, YOU'RE NOW WORKING FOR THE LAW! DON'T FORGET THAT!

I WON'T -- UNLESS I GET AMNESIA AGAIN! I WAS SCARED, BUT NOT ANYMORE... NOT WHILE MOUSEY IS SAFELY LOCKED UP!

BUT IS HE? FOR AS SOON AS THE FURTIVE LITTLE CROOK IS ALONE IN HIS CELL...

HA, HA... LUCKY THOSE COPPERS DIDN'T FIND THIS FILE HIDDEN IN MY SHOE! ONCE I GET OUT, IT'LL BE BYE-BYE CATWOMAN!

EACH RASP OF THE FILE IS LIKE THE TICK OF A CLOCK... AND WITH EACH PASSING MOMENT, DEATH LOOMS CLOSER FOR SELINA KYLE -- ALIAS THE CATWOMAN!

47

MISSED, *BLAST 'EM!* THEY KEEP HOPPING AROUND!

TIME FOR ME TO GO INTO ACTION!

MOMENTS LATER, A LENGTHENED *CAT-O'-NINE-TAILS* SNAPS OUT AT THE MASKED LAWMEN, AND...

HEY! *CATWOMAN* GOT 'EM FROM THE *CATWALK!* START SHOOTIN', BOYS.'

NO! DON'T SHOOT! I WANT THEM *ALIVE!*

HUH? WHAT'S WHAT'S THE MATTER *CATWOMAN?* GOIN' SOFT!?

FOOLS! MY DEAL WITH *MISTER X* DIDN'T INCLUDE THE CAPTURE OF *BATMAN* AND *ROBIN!* I WANT A *BONUS* FOR THIS, AND I DON'T TALK BUSINESS TILL I SEE *MISTER X IN PERSON!*

OKAY! THIS IS IMPORTANT ENOUGH FOR ME TO CONTACT HIM!

YOUR PLAN'S WORKING, *BATMAN!* AT LAST, WE'RE GOING TO MEET *MISTER X!*

YES, *ROBIN*, BUT WE MUST REMAIN CAREFUL... LETTING OURSELVES BE "CAPTURED" IS ONLY HALF THE JOB! FROM NOW ON, ONE SLIPUP, AND WE'RE DEAD DUCKS!

AT THAT MOMENT, IN MOUSEY'S CELL...

AHH.. TWO BARS OUT--ONE TO GO! IT WON'T BE LONG NOW-- SOON, IT'S GONNA BE CURTAINS FOR THE *CATWOMAN!*

AND WILL IT ALSO BE CURTAINS FOR *BATMAN* AND *ROBIN?* FOR IF THE *CATWOMAN* DIES, THE PLAN TO RESCUE *BATMAN* AND *ROBIN* DIES WITH HER!

HOURS LATER, IN A DESERTED FARMHOUSE ON THE OUTSKIRTS OF GOTHAM CITY...

DIPPER EXPLAINED EVERYTHING, *CATWOMAN!* YOU DID A FINE JOB! BOYS, TAKE THEIR UTILITY BELTS AWAY--I'VE GOT PLANS FOR *BATMAN* AND *ROBIN!*

AND WE'VE GOT PLANS FOR YOU, TOO, *MISTER X!*

JUST THEN...

OH! MY CAT IS STILL ANGRY OVER THAT FAKE MOUSE! COME BACK, KITTY... YOU'RE HURTING THE NICE MAN!

HURTING HIM? I WONDER..?

GET RID OF THIS LITTLE MONSTER!

WAIT! THAT SPINDLY OLD CHAIR! NOW I KNOW MY HUNCH IS RIGHT!

OKAY, JOE, AL--LOCK UP BATMAN AND ROBIN IN THAT OLD GRAIN MILL-- AND PLANT A TIME BOMB THERE! THE ONLY WAY THEY'LL GET OUT IS BY BEING BLOWN OUT!

OH, DEAR... HOW WILL I SAVE THEM?

SOON, IN MISTER X'S MAKESHIFT PRISON...

UHH! THIS DOOR'S LOCKED SOLID! IT WON'T BUDGE!

AND THERE'S A TIME BOMB SET TO GO OFF ANY MINUTE! THE CATWOMAN HAD BETTER NOT FAIL US-- OR WE'RE GONERS!

BUT AT THAT INSTANT, WHEN THE CATWOMAN TRIES TO ACT...

AHA...JUST AS I EXPECTED! SHE WAS ABOUT TO THROW THIS GLASS VIAL-- PROBABLY LOADED WITH KNOCKOUT GAS! GRAB HER, BOYS.

BUT... BUT HOW DID YOU KNOW?

HUH? I DON'T GET IT, BOSS-- BUT YOU'RE GIVIN' THE ORDERS!

MINUTES LATER...

TOO BAD, CATWOMAN... MOUSEY ESCAPED FROM JAIL AND LET ME IN ON YOUR WHOLE SCHEME! NOW, YOU'RE DOOMED! AFTER WE TIE YOU TO THIS TRACTOR, WE'LL SEND YOU HURTLING OVER THAT CLIFF! HA, HA!

WITH BOTH BATMAN, ROBIN AND THE CATWOMAN FACING DEATH, WHAT WILL HAPPEN NOW! HOW CAN THEY POSSIBLY BE SAVED?

THEN, BEFORE THE STARTLED THUGS CAN TURN...

DIPPER HAS DROPPED! BATMAN--THERE GOES MISTER X! HE'S GETTING AWAY!

BUT AS THE MASKED GANG CHIEF PASSES THE CATWOMAN...

THANKS FOR THE HAND, CATWOMAN! AHH--I HAD A HUNCH MISTER X WAS A SHORT MAN!

SHORT MAN?! WHY, MISTER X IS MOUSEY!!

I SEE... HE WORE A WOODEN FRAME TO MAKE HIM LOOK BIGGER!

I REALIZED MISTER X WAS ONLY MASQUERADING AS A BIG MAN BECAUSE HIS FLIMSY CHAIR DIDN'T CREAK OR BREAK UNDER HIS WEIGHT! HE DIDN'T YELL WHEN THE CAT WAS CLAWING HIS LEG, SO I GUESSED HE WAS WEARING WOODEN STILTS!

LATER, MOUSEY EXPLAINS THE REASON FOR HIS DISGUISE...

FIRST, IT WAS A GOOD COVERUP! THE COPS WOULD BE HUNTING FOR MISTER X, NOT A PUNK NAMED MOUSEY! YEAH... MY NAME... MOUSEY ... THAT WAS THE REAL REASON FOR EVERYTHING...

NO GANGSTERS WOULD TAKE ORDERS FROM A LITTLE GUY THEY CALL MOUSEY. IN THE UNDERWORLD, YOU HAVE TO BE IMPRESSIVE! SO, BY POSING AS A MYSTERY MAN --A BIG MAN-- I GOT MYSELF A GANG! MOUSEY, THE PUNK, BECAME MISTER X, THE BIG SHOT!

YES, MOUSEY, YOU'LL BE THE BIGGEST MAN IN PRISON!

AND SO, AT POLICE HEADQUARTERS!

THAT'S THAT! FROM NOW ON I'M PLAIN SELINA KYLE! THE CATWOMAN HAS RETIRED!

I WONDER! SOMEHOW, I THINK THE LAW WILL AGAIN NEED THE SERVICES OF CATWOMAN-- POLICE OPERATIVE... AND IT MAY BE SOONER THAN YOU THINK!

THE END

Written by Edmond Hamilton/Art by Lew Sayre Schwartz & Charles Paris

THE RELEASE OF A NOTORIOUS CONVICT BRINGS FAMED CRIME-FIGHTERS *BATMAN* AND *ROBIN* ON A SPECIAL VISIT TO STATE PRISON...

YES, *THE PENGUIN* IS BEING RELEASED TODAY, AND HE SAYS HE'S REALLY GOING STRAIGHT THIS TIME! HE'S BEEN STUDYING UP SOME PROJECT ABOUT BIRDS!

OH, OH--THAT'S NOT SO GOOD, WARDEN! WHEN THE PENGUIN RIDES HIS BIRD HOBBY, IT'S USUALLY FOR *CRIME!*

BUT THE LITTLE BIRD-BANDIT SEEMS IN EARNEST ABOUT REFORM THIS TIME...

YES, *BATMAN*, I'M THROUGH WITH CRIME! SOON I SHALL ASTOUND THE WORLD IN A LEGAL MANNER! MY VAST KNOWLEDGE OF BIRD LORE CONVINCES ME THAT MANY FABULOUS BIRDS OF THE PAST--THE *PHOENIX*, THE *BASILISK*, AND SO ON REALLY EXISTED!

BUT THAT'S IMPOSSIBLE, PENGUIN!

HMPH! YOU MAY LAUGH, MY FRIEND, BUT I BELIEVE SPECIMENS OF THOSE FABULOUS BIRDS STILL EXIST IN REMOTE PARTS OF THE WORLD--AND I SHALL GO FIND THEM.

SOUNDS CRAZY TO ME--BUT IF IT KEEPS YOU OUT OF TROUBLE, GO RIGHT AHEAD!

SO THE PENGUIN DROPS OUT OF SIGHT, WHILE *BATMAN* AND *ROBIN* IN THEIR EVERYDAY IDENTITIES OF WEALTHY BRUCE WAYNE AND HIS YOUNG WARD DICK GRAYSON, GET A WELCOME REST...

...TILL ONE MORNING SHORTLY AFTERWARD..

DO YOU SUPPOSE THE PENGUIN REALLY WENT ON THAT WHACKY QUEST FOR LEGENDARY BIRDS, BRUCE?

I CAN'T SAY, DICK--BUT WHEREVER HE IS, I HOPE HE STAYS THERE!

FLASH! WE INTERRUPT THIS PROGRAM WITH A SPECIAL NEWS BULLETIN.

THE PENGUIN HAS JUST ARRIVED AT GOTHAM CITY HARBOR IN A CHARTERED SCHOONER AND HAS PROMISED TO MAKE A SENSATIONAL ANNOUNCEMENT!

I KNEW THIS QUIET WAS TOO GOOD TO LAST! GET INTO YOUR COSTUME, DICK... IT'S UP TO *BATMAN* AND *ROBIN* TO FIND OUT WHAT THAT LITTLE SCHEMER IS PLANNING NOW!

AND IT'S INDEED A SENSATIONAL ANNOUNCEMENT THAT GREETS THE TWO LAWMEN WHEN THEY REACH THE DOCK...

YES, GENTLEMEN, I'VE SUCCEEDED IN MY QUEST FOR THE BIRDS OF LEGEND! THE *ROC*, THE *PHOENIX*... I HAVE SPECIMENS OF THEM ALL IN THESE SPECIAL AIR-CONDITIONED CASES!

BUT THOSE BIRDS WERE ALWAYS CONSIDERED MYTHICAL! LET'S SEE ONE OF THEM!

BASILISK

PHOENIX

CERTAINLY NOT! I INTEND TO MAKE A FORTUNE EXHIBITING MY LEGENDARY BIRDS, SO I'LL NOT SHOW THEM NOW AND SPOIL MY SHOW! I'M TAKING THEM TO MY NEW COUNTRY-PLACE AVIARY!

AND WHAT'S IN THE CASE MARKED "MYSTERY BIRD"?

THAT'S MY STRANGEST LEGENDARY BIRD OF ALL... A BIRD THAT WOULD DESTROY YOUR CAREER IF I RELEASED IT, BATMAN! BUT I WON'T--FOR I'M A LAW-ABIDING CITIZEN NOW!

DESTROY BATMAN'S CAREER WITH A BIRD? THAT'S RIDICULOUS...THIS WHOLE BUSINESS SOUNDS LIKE A BIG BLUFF!

BUT THOUGH SKEPTICAL REPORTERS CONSIDER IT A BLUFF, BATMAN DOES NOT DISMISS THE PENGUIN SO LIGHTLY...

THIS WEIRD LEGENDARY BIRD MAY COVER UP SOME CRIME HE'S HATCHING! WE'LL GO TAKE A LOOK AT HIS COUNTRY AVIARY TONIGHT, ROBIN!

GOOD IDEA, BATMAN...I WON'T BELIEVE A THING UNTIL I SEE THOSE CREATURES WITH MY OWN EYES!

BUT THAT NIGHT, AS A STORM BUILDS OVER THE COUNTRYSIDE, THE CAPED CRIME-CRUSHERS FIND THE PENGUIN'S NEST BESET BY HUMAN BIRDS OF PREY!

FOR ONCE I'M GLAD TO SEE YOU, BATMAN! ENRAGED CROOKS HAVE JUST SET LOOSE MY FABULOUS BIRDS, BECAUSE I WAS UNWILLING TO RESUME MY LIFE OF CRIME WITH THEM!

WHAT--?

THERE THEY GO NOW!

THEY SIDESWIPED THE BATMOBILE, TO PREVENT US FROM FOLLOWING! ROBIN, USE THE POWER-HOIST TO PULL IT OUT WHILE I TAKE A LOOK AT THE PENGUIN'S CAGES!

WHRROOM!

③

SOB! THEY RELEASED THEM! MY FABULOUS BIRDS ARE GONE-- AND THEY'RE DANGEROUS! THE WINGED LION, THE GIANT THUNDERBIRD, THE HUGE BASILISK--THEY'LL ENDANGER ALL GOTHAM CITY!

IF THEY REALLY EXIST!

BUT BATMAN'S SKEPTICISM IS DUE FOR A STUNNING SURPRISE...

SHORTLY, OUTSIDE...

YES, A LOT OF CASH WAS LOST IN THE FIRE!

I DIDN'T TAKE IT! YOU SEARCHED ME AGAIN, DIDN'T YOU?

I DID, PENGUIN, BUT I'M STILL NOT SATISFIED! I'M ARRESTING YOU ON SUSPICION OF ROBBERY!

AWHILE LATER, AT POLICE HEADQUARTERS...

BUT THESE FABULOUS BIRDS HAVE BEEN SEEN BY THE WHOLE CITY, BATMAN! THEY'RE REAL!

MAYBE, COMMISSIONER GORDON -- BUT UNTIL WE CATCH THEM, I WANT THIS BIRD KEPT IN A CAGE!

HA, HA... MY HENCHMEN WILL SEE THAT MY BASILISK GETS ME OUT! BATMAN WILL LOSE HIS WITS TRYING TO SOLVE THE SECRET OF MY BIRDS!

AFTERWARDS, AS BATMAN AND ROBIN MAINTAIN A TENSE VIGIL...

EACH TIME THE PENGUIN'S FABULOUS BIRDS WREAKED DESTRUCTION, SOMETHING VALUABLE'S BEEN MISSING! IT COULD BE COINCIDENCE, BUT...

OH, OH... THERE'S SOME SORT OF COMMOTION OVER ON 34TH STREET! LET'S GO, BATMAN!

IT'S MORE THAN MERE COMMOTION THAT GREETS THE CAPED CRIME-BUSTERS AS THEY REACH 34TH STREET...

THAT HORRIBLE MONSTER... ITS EYES ARE FREEZING ME! I CAN'T MOVE!

IT'S THE LEGENDARY BASILISK -- THE GIANT BIRD WHOSE EYES CAN FREEZE A MAN!

AND AS A HORROR OUT OF ANCIENT TRADITION STALKS THE STREETS, FRANTIC REPORTS REACH HEADQUARTERS...

TERRIBLE BIRD ON 34TH STREET -- MANY PEOPLE ALREADY FROZEN BY ITS STARE! OFFICER MANTON TRIED TO FACE IT BUT WAS FROZEN TOO...

IT'S MY ESCAPED BASILISK! I CAN CATCH IT -- LET ME OUT BEFORE IT STRIKES DOWN MORE PEOPLE!

PENGUIN, IF YOU CAN HANDLE THAT HORRIBLE BIRD, CATCH IT AT ONCE! NO ONE ELSE CAN FACE IT!

I DID WRONG TO BRING MY FABULOUS FOWLS TO GOTHAM CITY -- BUT I'LL RECAPTURE THEM, COMMISSIONER!

SECONDS LATER...

FOR YOUR INTERFERENCE, *BATMAN*, I'LL RELEASE MY *MYSTERY BIRD*, WHICH WILL RUIN YOUR CAREER!

CAN'T WORRY ABOUT THAT NOW, PENGUIN ...THAT RUN-AWAY BUS IS MORE IMPORTANT!

I CAN STOP THE BUS NOW, *BATMAN*, BUT I'M AFRAID THE PENGUIN FLEW THE COOP!

EVEN IN MID-AIR, YOU *WOULD* MAKE PUNS!

ACME TRANSIT CO. 943

NEXT MORNING, IN A SECRET WAREHOUSE BASE, AN ANGRY PENGUIN PREPARES TO LOOSE HIS MOST FABULOUS BIRD...

MY *MYSTERY BIRD* WILL TURN THE WHOLE CITY *AGAINST BATMAN*! THEN WE'LL USE THE *ROC* FOR OUR STADIUM RAID, AND GET OUT OF TOWN!

WE SURE FOOLED HIM WHEN WE PRE-TENDED TO RELEASE ALL YOUR OTHER BIRDS! WHAT A GAG!

ROC

MYSTERY BIRD

FRAGILE

A LITTLE LATER...

LOOK--THERE'S *BATMAN*! HE MUST BE SWINGING DOWN ON HIS ROPE!

GEE--HE LOOKS LIKE HE'S *FLYING*!

WHILE IN THE SECRET *BAT-CAVE* BENEATH THE WAYNE MANSION...

ROBIN, YOU TAKE THE *BAT-PLANE* AND PATROL THE SKY FOR THE PENGUIN'S *BIRDS*... I'LL USE THE *BATMOBILE* ON THE GROUND, AND CALL YOU BY BELT-RADIO IF I NEED YOU!

GOOD IDEA, *BATMAN*!

WAIT A MINUTE-- HE *IS* FLYING! THAT'S NOT *BATMAN*...IT'S SOME SORT OF BATLIKE CREATURE... A *MAN-BAT*!

IT'S GHASTLY! RUN!

⑧

BUT **BATMAN**, FOR THE FIRST TIME, SOON FINDS THE PEOPLE OF GOTHAM CITY FLEEING FROM HIM IN TERROR!

RUN! IT'S THAT AWFUL **MAN-BAT!** GET AWAY!

MAN-BAT? SO THAT'S THE MYSTERY BIRD THE PENGUIN THREATENED ME WITH? IT **COULD** DESTROY MY CAREER, BY MAKING PEOPLE AFRAID OF ME WHEREVER I APPEAR!

AT THAT INSTANT, FROM HIGH IN THE SKY, COMES A TENSE CALL BY BELT-RADIO...

BATMAN, THERE'S A WEIRD MAN-LIKE BIRD FLYING OVER 9TH AVENUE!

I'LL STOP THAT **MAN-BAT!** YOU SWOOP DOWN AND LAND ON THE TERMINAL ROOF!

IMMEDIATELY, **BATMAN** RACES TO THE TOP OF A TALL SKYSCRAPER, AND ...

SMACK!

THE ONLY WAY TO STOP THIS THING IS BY FORCING IT DOWN TO THE GROUND!

INSTEAD OF BEING AWAY HUNTING FABULOUS BIRDS, HE WAS BUILDING THOSE FAKES! I KNEW THIS BECAUSE WHEN A **REAL** BIRD IS RELEASED FROM CAPTIVITY, IT ALWAYS FLIES HOME... BUT THESE "BIRDS" WENT STRAIGHT TO THE CITY AND BEGAN WREAKING HAVOC!

AND BY THE TIME **ROBIN** JOINS HIM...

SO THAT'S THE ANSWER. A **MECHANICAL**, MONSTROUS MAN-BAT!

RIGHT... **ALL** THE PENGUIN'S **BIRDS** ARE MECHANICAL FAKES -- THE "THUNDER-BIRD" THAT DREW LIGHTNING AND CARRIED AWAY THE ART-LOOT, THE "PHOENIX" WHICH FLEW AWAY WITH THE BANK-CASH, AND THE "BASILISK" THAT PRODUCED KNOCKOUT GAS!

SUDDENLY...

LOOK! THAT COLOSSAL BIRD SCREAMING OVER-HEAD! IT MUST BE...

SCREECH! SCREECH!

THE PENGUIN'S FAKE **ROC!** QUICK-- BACK TO THE **BAT-PLANE!**

NEXT MINUTE, OVER GOTHAM FOOTBALL STADIUM...

THAT MONSTER BIRD--IT'S SWOOPING DOWN ON US!

SCREEEEECH!

WATCH OUT!

HA, HA... THEY CAN'T SEE THE HELICOPTER BLADES FROM BENEATH, AND THE SIREN-SCREECHES DROWN OUT OUR MOTOR NOISE! IN THIS PANIC, WE CAN LAND AND GRAB ALL THE BOX-OFFICE RECEIPTS!

NO, PENGUIN-- LOOK ABOVE US! THE BAT-PLANE!

ROBIN, DROP THIS METAL MOORING-LINE IN THEIR PROPELLOR AS WE GO OVER THEM!

HURRAY! THE BAT-PLANE ...IT'S DIVING ON THE ROC!

PENGUIN! WE'RE GOING DOWN! IN THE STADIUM, WE CAN'T GET AWAY!

IT'S THAT DRATTED BATMAN! I THOUGHT MY MAN-BAT GAG WOULD KEEP HIM TOO BUSY TO INTERFERE!

AND SO, AFTER A SWIFT ROUNDUP...

POOR PENGUIN... THIS LATEST SCHEME OF HIS REALLY LAID AN EGG, DIDN'T IT?

OH-H...BAD ENOUGH, I'M GOING BACK TO JAIL... DO I HAVE TO LISTEN TO THAT BRAT'S HORRIBLE PUNS, TOO?

The END

10

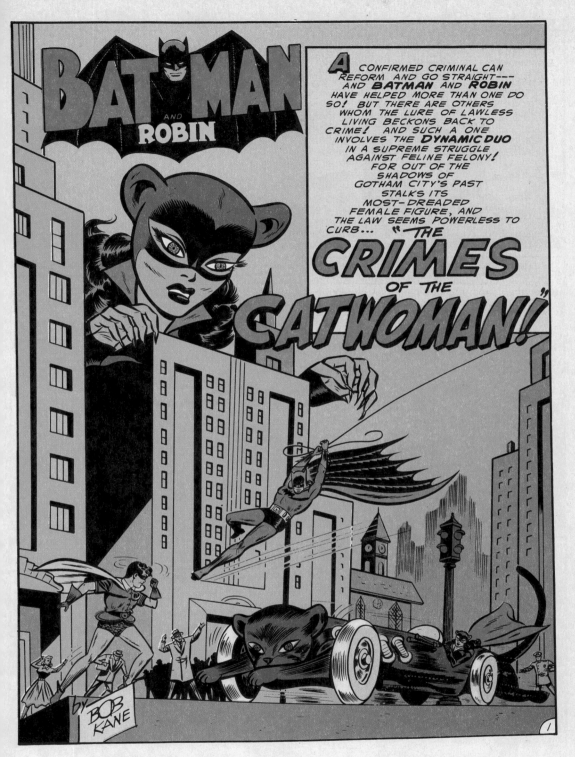

Written by Edmond Hamilton/Art by Lew Sayre Schwartz & Charles Paris/Lettering by Pat Gordon

TO BRUCE WAYNE AND HIS WARD, DICK GRAYSON, WHO ARE SECRETLY *BATMAN* AND *ROBIN*, THE *BOY WONDER*, THAT CRYPTIC SYMBOL MEANS BUT ONE THING!

THAT SIGN CAN ONLY MEAN THE *CATWOMAN* IS ON THE PROWL AGAIN!

HOW COULD SHE DO IT? I'VE DONE EVERYTHING TO KEEP HER AWAY FROM CRIME! TOO LATE NOW--- SHE'S CHOSEN HER PATH, AND WE HAVE TO STOP HER AT ANY COST!

IN THE *BATCAVE* BENEATH BRUCE WAYNE'S MANSION, A SWIFT SWITCH OF COSTUME--- AND THEN THE *BATPLANE* SOARS INTO THE NIGHT!

ROBIN, THE MAIL-HELICOPTER IS CARRYING A SHIPMENT OF VALUABLE IRIDIUM TONIGHT! I THINK WE'D BETTER WATCH IT! ANYWAY!

RIGHT-- IT'S THE KIND OF BAIT *CATWOMAN* WOULD STRIKE AT!

... THAT MY *CAT*-APULT CAN GET ME TO IT FAST---

THEY THINK THEIR MAIL-HELICOPTER IS SAFE WHEN IT'S CROSSING THE CITY TO THE AIRPORT, BUT THEY DON'T REALIZE---

CATWOMAN! WHAT--- HOW---

... AND THAT MY *CAT-OF-NINE-TAILS* CAN BIND THE PILOT TO HIS SEAT IN ONE WHIP OF THE LASH! NOW TO LAND ON A ROOF AND ESCAPE WITH THE IRIDIUM!

BUT KEEN EYES HAVE SEEN, AND DOWN FROM THE SKY HURTLES A DARK-WINGED NEMESIS SUPPORTED BY A SLENDER SILKEN CORD!

THAT MAIL-HELICOPTER WOULDN'T LAND ON THAT ROOF IF ALL WAS WELL--- THERE ISN'T ROOM TO LAND THE *BATPLANE* THERE, BUT I CAN MANAGE THIS SHORT DROP WITH MY SILKEN CORD!

4

AND HIGH ABOVE THE CITY, THE TWO GREAT ANTAGONISTS ONCE AGAIN CONFRONT EACH OTHER!

I LEFT THE PILOT TIED AND THE MOTOR'S RUNNING-- I KNOW YOU'LL MAKE SURE HE'S SAFE BEFORE YOU COME AFTER ME, BATMAN!

BUT YOU CAN'T ESCAPE FROM THIS ROOF! YOU MIGHT AS WELL SURRENDER, SELINA!

BUT AS BATMAN HASTILY STOPS THE HELICOPTER MOTOR, THE FELINE FELON HAS SWIFTLY FLUNG A ROPE TO THE NEXT ROOFTOP IN INTRICATE PATTERN!

I'M CATWOMAN NOW! AND A CAT'S-CRADLE MAKES A GOOD BRIDGE FOR ME, DON'T YOU THINK?

I'M FOLLOWING YOU FROM HERE ON!

I COULD HAVE WAITED TILL YOU WERE ON IT AND THEN DONE THIS, BATMAN... BUT THAT WOULD BE TOO CATTY A TRICK!

STILL THIS MANIA FOR CAT-CRIME TRICKS! YOU MAY ESCAPE BY USING ONE THIS TIME, BUT THEY'LL BRING YOU TO YOUR DOOM!

SOON, ACROSS A STARTLED CITY SPREADS THE SINISTER NEWS...

Daily CATWOMAN DARING MAIL

Times COMES BACK ROBBERY EXTRA

AND IN THE SHADOWY UNDERWORLD THERE IS NEW RESPECT FOR THE CATWOMAN!

SHE WAS TOO MUCH FOR BATMAN, ALL RIGHT! IF I COULD GET INTO HER GANG, I'D SURE DO IT!

THE RUMOR IS THAT SHE'S FITTED UP A NEW HIDEOUT--- A NEW CATACOMB!

YES, THE PRINCESS OF PLUNDER AGAIN HAS A SECRET LAIR WITH THE FELINE FURNISHINGS SHE LOVES!

THIS NEW CATACOMB IS EVEN SPLASHIER THAN YOUR OLD ONE, CATWOMAN!

YES, AND MY NEW KITTY CAR IS EVEN MORE POWERFUL! NOW I'LL MAKE GOTHAM CITY DREAD THE VERY NAME OF CAT--- AND THIS IS HOW WE'LL START!

5

MEANWHILE, A GRIM **BATMAN** PREPARES FOR A DEADLY DUEL! IN POLICE COMMISSIONER GORDON'S OFFICE...

BATMAN, YOU SEEMED SO INTERESTED IN THIS GIRL, THE WAY YOU TRIED TO GET HER TO GO STRAIGHT--- PERHAPS YOU'D RATHER STAY OUT OF THIS **CATWOMAN** CASE?

NO, I TRIED TO HELP HER, BUT SHE CHOSE TO RETURN TO CRIME! I MUST BRING HER TO JUSTICE!

BUT HOW CAN WE TELL WHERE SHE'LL STRIKE NEXT?

SHE ALWAYS SPECIALIZES IN **CAT** CRIMES. NOW LOOK AT THESE TWO ITEMS--- ONE ABOUT GUY VANEY, THE LION-TAMER AT THE GOTHAM GARDEN CIRCUS! THE OTHER ABOUT HORACE BRAHAM, MILLIONAIRE COLLECTOR OF CAT'S-EYE JEWELS!

I GET IT--- A LION-TAMER IS A "CAT" MAN, IN SHOW SLANG!

YES, AND THAT'S WHY I'M GOING TO GOTHAM GARDEN! **ROBIN,** YOU WARN BRAHAM TO GET HIS CAT'S-EYE JEWEL COLLECTION TO SOME SAFE PLACE!

SOON, BENEATH THE GREAT ROOF OF GOTHAM GARDEN, AS A CAPACITY CROWD WATCHES A BREATH-TAKING LION ACT!

MEEEOOW

THOSE LION-SNARLS MAKE ECHOES FROM THE CEILING THAT SOUND LIKE CAT-SNARLS!

THOSE AREN'T ECHOES--- THEY SOUND LIKE REAL CAT-CRIES! **CATWOMAN** MUST BE USING CATS UP THERE IN SOME CRIME-PLAN!

SWIFTLY, UNSUSPECTED BY THE AUDIENCE, THE **BATMAN** CLIMBS HIGH INTO THE NETWORK OF GIRDERS THAT SUPPORT THE ROOF!

I THOUGHT SHE MIGHT USE REAL CATS, AND BROUGHT CATNIP IN MY UTILITY-BELT TO DIVERT THEM IN CASE--- BUT WHAT'S THIS?

MEEOWW

MEEOWW MEEOW MEEOWW

THEY'RE NOT CATS BUT **CATBIRDS**--- BIRDS THAT UTTER A REALISTIC CAT-LIKE CALL! SHE TURNED THEM LOOSE SO THEY'D LEAD A FALSE TRAIL UP HERE!

6

TAKE IT EASY, *CATWOMAN!* YOU'LL KILL US BEFORE WE EVER REACH YOUR HIDEOUT!

FOOLS--- OUR SPEED IS OUR ONLY SAFETY!

HONK

WHEN CONSCIOUSNESS RETURNS TO THE *BATMAN...*

I'M STILL DREAMING--- THAT FACE---

NO, *BATMAN!* IT'S REAL!

MY LITTLE PETS SEEM TO LIKE YOU!

SO THIS IS THE NEW *CATACOMB!* BUT HOW DID I--- NOW I REMEMBER--- THE GOTHAM GARDEN--- THE GAS I DETECTED TOO LATE!

NOT TOO LATE TO SAVE THE BOX-OFFICE FUND THERE--- YOU LOCKED THE SAFE IN TIME! BUT TOO LATE TO SAVE YOURSELF!

SO YOU BROUGHT ME HERE, INSTEAD OF LETTING YOUR THUGS MURDER ME--- WHY?

ONLY BECAUSE YOU'RE A VALUABLE HOSTAGE! NOW WE'RE GOING TO PICK UP SOME REMARKABLE CAT'S-EYE JEWELS--- AND I'LL LEAVE YOU SAFELY TIED WITH MY PETS TO KEEP YOU COMPANY!

SO SHE'S AFTER HORACE BRAHAM'S JEWELS, AS I THOUGHT! IF *ROBIN* WARNED BRAHAM, AND IF BRAHAM HEEDED THE WARNING, SHE'LL BE DISAPPOINTED!

At the mansion of the millionaire collector...

IF *CATWOMAN* IS AFTER MY CAT'S-EYE COLLECTION, I'LL BE SAFEST WITH IT ON MY YACHT ANCHORED IN MID-RIVER!

WE'LL KEEP AN EYE ON YOUR YACHT, AS SOON AS I CONTACT AND PICK UP *BATMAN!*

8

SOON...

I CALLED COMMISSIONER GORDON--- HE SAID THE PEOPLE AT GOTHAM GARDEN SOON RECOVERED FROM THE KNOCKOUT GAS, AND THAT YOU'D PREVENTED THE ROBBERY THERE!

BUT CATWOMAN'S CATBIRD TRICK WAS ALMOST TOO MUCH FOR ME!

THOSE ANGRY CROOKS WOULD SURELY HAVE KILLED YOU IF SHE HADN'T INTERVENED, BATMAN! IT'S STRANGE, HER FEELING TOWARD YOU!

NO USE TALKING ABOUT THAT--- SHE'S GOT TO BE STOPPED! I ONLY HOPE WE'RE NOT TOO LATE AT BRAHAM'S YACHT!

HORACE BRAHAM FEELS PERFECTLY SAFE--- ALTHOUGH A BIT BORED!

YOU CREWMEN KEEP A LOOKOUT FOR ANY BOAT THAT TRIES TO APPROACH US!

YES, MR. BRAHAM!

HA, HA--- CATS DON'T LIKE WATER AND CATWOMAN CAN'T BOTHER MY CAT'S-EYES HERE! I'LL DO A LITTLE FISHING UNTIL THE BATMAN GETS THIS FEMALE FELINE UNDER ARREST!

BUT A LITTLE WAY UPRIVER, CRYPTIC PREPARATIONS ARE BEING SWIFTLY MADE!

BRAHAM'S SUCH AN AVID ANGLER, I KNEW HE'D BE FISHING --- AND I'M GOING TO USE THAT FACT TO GET ABOARD HIS YACHT! YOU BE READY TO PICK ME UP WHEN I HAVE THE JEWELS!

WE'LL BE WATCHING!

AND A MOMENT LATER...

THERE SHE GOES-- AND BRAHAM HAS GOT A SURPRISE COMING!

10

Yes, the **PRINCESS OF PLUNDER** can still show her claws!

I may not get those **CAT'S-EYES**, but by **CUTTING THE ANCHOR**, raising it to the **CATHEAD**, I can keep you busy!

BATMAN, the yacht's drifting into the path of that liner!

Bye, bye-- **BATMAN**--I can use one of those moored **CATBOATS** to get away in!

She wrecked the control so we can't drop anchor again! We're drifting into the liner!

If I can use this **POWER-LAUNCH** to push the yacht out of the way!

Powerful marine motors roar, struggling to avert a catastrophic collision...

We're clear, **BATMAN**--- and now that we're getting our engines started, we'll be safe!

And **ROBIN** and I will run down **CATWOMAN**--- though her catboat has a start on us!

THE GRIM PURSUIT RACES OUT OF THE RIVER INTO THE STORMY OUTER SEA!

BATMAN, look--- the waves were too much for her little catboat--- it was wrecked on that marshy shore!

We'll run in there--- we might still be in time!

But in the reed-grown, marshy waters...

We've searched this whole marsh, and no sign of her body--- it must have been swept back out to sea! Well--- she brought her fate on herself, but I still feel badly!

I might, too, if I were sure of her fate, but---

12

--- It's more likely she used one of these hollow **CAT-TAIL** reeds to breathe through, and escaped underwater unseen!

Living, or dead? Only time will tell about the **CATWOMAN**!

THE END

Written by France Eddie Herron/Art by Sheldon Moldoff & Joe Giella

THIS IS THE HIDE-OUT OF THE *PENGUIN*--PAUNCHY, MONOCLED, CULPRIT KNOWN AS *THE MAN OF 1000 UMBRELLAS*...

HOW IRRITATING! NOW THAT I'VE SERVED MY SENTENCE AND AM FREE TO OPERATE AGAIN --I CAN'T THINK OF A *SINGLE* CRIME WORTHY OF MY TALENTS --OR MY UMBRELLAS!

YES--AND SOMETHING WORTHY OF *BATMAN'S* METTLE, TOO! NO HUMDRUM ROBBERIES! I WANT A CLEVER CRIME-- *SENSATIONAL*...SEETHING WITH THE *UNEXPECTED*! MAYBE I'M WASHED UP...

AH,...WHAT A *BIRD-BRAIN* I'VE BEEN! NO WONDER MY MIND'S A BARREN WILDERNESS! I NEED AN *UMBRELLA* FOR INSPIRATION!

ALREADY THOUGHTS WING IN... AND I'VE GOT IT--THE SCHEME OF THE CENTURY! *BATMAN* HIMSELF WILL NOT ONLY *SELECT* MY CRIME -- BUT WILL *BLUEPRINT* ITS OPERATION FOR ME!

I'LL LAUNCH A BIZARRE, SENSELESS *UMBRELLA BARRAGE* ON *GOTHAM CITY*--"SENSELESS" TO ALL BUT *BATMAN*, WHOSE KEEN MIND WILL PIECE TOGETHER THE CLUES TO MY "CRIME"! TOMORROW WILL BE *U-DAY-- U-* FOR *UMBRELLA*! HA! HA!

NINE-THIRTY THE NEXT MORNING, AROUND THE CORNER FROM A JEWELRY STORE HOLDING ITS GRAND OPENING...

A DRAWING FOR PRIZES WILL BE HELD IN THE JEWELRY STORE AT 10:00 SHARP!

CARRY AN UMBRELLA INSIDE! MAYBE *YOURS* WILL BE THE LUCKY ONE!

HERE YOU ARE, FOLKS! GET YOUR *FREE* UMBRELLAS! MAYBE *YOU* WILL WIN ... OR *YOU*!

GRAND OPENING!

2

SHORTLY, INSIDE THE STORE...

WONDER WHAT EVERYBODY'S DOING WITH AN UMBRELLA ON A NICE DAY LIKE THIS... WEATHER REPORT DIDN'T MENTION RAIN...

AND AT TEN SHARP...

HEY! MY UMBRELLA OPENED BY ITSELF!

SO DID MINE! WHAT'S GOIN' ON?

SNAP!

SNAP!

CRACKLE!!

HELP! THESE UMBRELLAS ARE ACTING UP... SHOOTING OUT SMOKE, LIGHTNING--!

CALL THE POLICE!

SALE

THE POLICE ARRIVE--ON THE DOUBLE...

I DON'T KNOW WHAT HAPPENED! EVERYBODY CAME IN WITH UMBRELLAS--THEN THAT WILD ACTION STARTED! NOPE-- NOBODY TRIED TO ROB US...

SOON, COMMISSIONER GORDON IS ON THE HOT-LINE WITH BATMAN...

BETTER HOP OVER TO HEADQUARTERS, BATMAN! I THINK THE PENGUIN'S UP TO SOME NEW UMBRELLA TRICKS!

WE'LL BE RIGHT THERE, COMMISSIONER.

3

AT 10:15, IN FRONT OF A BANK ACROSS TOWN...

MAKING A DEPOSIT, SIR? THAT'S *ALWAYS* GOOD FOR A RAINY DAY--AND SO IS THIS FREE UMBRELLA! MY COMPLIMENTS!

UH-- THANK YOU!

GOTHAM BANK

AS THE *BATMOBILE* WENDS ITS WAY THROUGH THE STREETS--THE *HOT-LINE* PHONE AGAIN...

BATMAN! A PATROLMAN SPOTTED ANOTHER MAN GIVING AWAY UMBRELLAS AT THE BANK ON JEFFERSON AND SEVENTH!

I GET YOU, COMMISSIONER! WE'LL GO STRAIGHT TO THE BANK!

FOR A BRIEF SPELL, THE FREE UMBRELLAS CARRIED INTO THE BANK SEEM HARMLESS ENOUGH--BUT, SUDDENLY...

SNAP! SNAP!

SNAP!

AND INTO THE SCENE OF BERSERK UMBRELLAS RUSH *BATMAN* AND *ROBIN*...

WOW! LOOKS LIKE FIGHTER PLANES IN A DOGFIGHT!

POP!

BUT NO SIGN OF THE *PENGUIN!* LET'S HAUL THOSE UMBRELLAS DOWN!

ZOOOOOOM!

BRATAT!!

*I*N A WILD SCRAMBLE, THE *GOTHAM CRIME-FIGHTERS* TANGLE WITH THE STRANGEST "ENEMY" THEY'VE EVER FOUGHT--*UMBRELLAS!*

GOT TWO OF THEM-- IT'S LIKE WRESTLING WITH FLYING EELS!

I JUST PUT ANOTHER ONE OUT OF ACTION!

FINALLY...

WE KNOW THE *PENGUIN'S* BEHIND THIS, BUT...

BUT *WHY?* WHAT'S HE UP TO? WHAT'S HIS GAME *THIS* TIME? WE'D BETTER HAVE A CHAT WITH THAT CAGEY LITTLE BIRD! HE BRAZENLY LEFT HIS ADDRESS ON THE UMBRELLAS!

4

AT THE *PENGUIN'S* UMBRELLA SHOP...

BATMAN NO DOUBT GOT WORD OF MY JEWELRY STORE CAPER--THEN THE ONE AT THE BANK HE'LL COME HERE...! BUT MY OTHER UMBRELLAS EN ROUTE SHOULD GIVE HIM A STORMY TIME FIRST!

THE WADDLING LITTLE CROOK IS *SO* RIGHT!

KA-PATTA

KA-PATTA

LOOK OUT! MORE WILD UMBRELLAS! THEY MIGHT *EXPLODE!*

RUNAWAY UMBRELLAS! LET'S USE OUR *ROPE BATARANGS!*

THE BAT-ARANGS WHIRL TO THEIR MARK...

WE'RE SLOWING 'EM DOWN!

NOTHING *ELSE* SPECIAL ABOUT THESE UMBRELLAS! THEY WERE SIMPLY RIGGED TO ROLL ALONG LIKE JUGGERNAUT WHEELS! *WHY?*

BATMAN! OVER THERE! *LOOK!*

A GREAT SHADOW FALLS OVER *GOTHAM SQUARE* AS...

A HUGE UMBRELLA-- DRIFTING DOWNWARD-- IN REVERSE! IT'S LIKE A *...FLYING SAUCER!*

STAY BACK, EVERY-BODY!

WHEN THE MYSTERY-UMBRELLA LANDS...

NO HIDDEN GIMMICKS ON *THIS* ONE, EITHER! BUT WE'VE GOT ENOUGH TO SLAP THE *PENGUIN* BEHIND BARS...OBSTRUCTING TRAFFIC...DISTURBING THE PEACE--AND SO FORTH!

YES,...WE CAN NAIL HIM BE-FORE HE PULLS HIS BIG PAY-OFF,... WHAT*EVER* IT IS!

BUT ALREADY THE WILY KING OF UMBRELLAS AWAITS THE DARING DUO...

TEN-FIVE! *BATMAN* WILL BE HERE IN ONE MINUTE--SO DIS-APPEAR, HERBIE! I HOPE *HE'S* FIGURED UNUSUAL WAYS TO PROFIT BY MY UMBRELLA GIMMICKS-- BECAUSE *I* HAVEN'T! Hmmm-- FIRST--TO SWITCH MY MONOCLE TO MY LEFT EYE...!

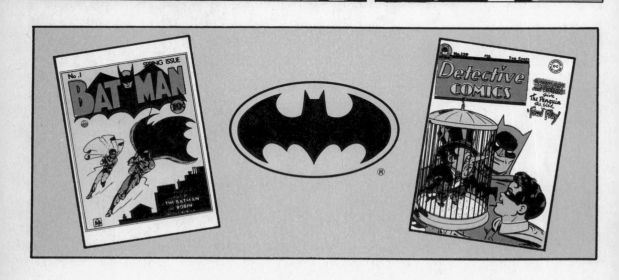

EXACTLY SIXTY SECONDS PASS AND THE CRIME-FIGHTERS ENTER THE PENGUIN'S SHOP...

AH! *BATMAN* AND *ROBIN*! SUCH DISTINGUISHED CUSTOMERS! MAY I SHOW YOU MY WARES?

WE'RE NOT HERE TO BUY UMBRELLAS, *PENGUIN*--AND YOU KNOW IT! WE'RE "FLYING" YOU DOWN TO HEADQUARTERS!

WE HAVE ENOUGH COUNTS AGAINST YOU AND YOUR UMBRELLAS TO PUT YOU ON ICE!

TUT-TUT, *BATMAN*! I HEARD THOSE WILD REPORTS ABOUT MY UMBRELLAS ON THE RADIO... I MEAN THE UMBRELLAS THAT HAD *BEEN* MINE!

YOU SEE, I MERELY *SELL* UMBRELLAS! WHAT HAPPENS TO THEM AFTER THEY *LEAVE* HERE IS NOT MY CONCERN, IN SHORT, YOU HAVEN'T A SCRAP OF EVIDENCE AGAINST ME!

AH! THEY'RE STARING AT MY WRONG-EYE MONOCLE! I *KNEW* IT WOULD GET THEM!

TRUE ENOUGH ABOUT LACK OF EVIDENCE, *PENGUIN*! YOU *COULD* HAVE TRIED A JOB AT THE JEWELER'S OR THE BANK--DURING THE CONFUSION...BUT DIDN'T! WELL, WE KNOW YOU'RE UP TO *SOMETHING*-- AND WE'LL BE WATCHING YOU!

WHEN ONCE AGAIN IN THE *BATMOBILE*...

I'M *CONVINCED* THE PENGUIN'S BEHIND ALL THIS MYSTERY, AND THINGS HAVE *GOT* TO COME TO A HEAD, SOONER OR LATER!

AND WHAT ABOUT HIS *MONOCLE*? HE ALWAYS WORE IT IN HIS *RIGHT* EYE--BUT NOW IT'S IN HIS *LEFT*!

7

YES--THAT **WAS** CURIOUS! I WONDER IF THE MONOCLE HAS ANYTHING TO DO WITH THIS PUZZLER? IT'S SUCH A WHACKY CASE I CAN BELIEVE **ANYTHING** WILL HAPPEN!

LET'S JUST HOPE WE'RE ON HAND WHEN IT DOES!

MEANWHILE...

TELL ME, BOSS--WHY **DID** YOU MOVE YOUR MONOCLE TO THE OTHER EYE?

JUST STRATEGY, HERBIE! IT'S A LITTLE SOMETHING **ELSE** THAT'LL KEEP **BATMAN** GUESSING-- KEEP HIM WORRIED! THAT'S THE **ONLY** REASON I DID IT! NOW--

I THINK TONIGHT WILL BE **THE** BIG NIGHT! SUMMON THE REST OF THE **BOYS** HERE AT ONCE! WE MUST WORK FAST-- ON THE BIGGEST PLAN OF MY LIFE--AND THE BIGGEST UPSET **BATMAN** EVER GOT!

LATE THAT NIGHT, FROM THE PROWLING **BATMOBILE**, THE CRIME-FIGHTERS SEE A STRANGE AND FASCINATING GLOW ABOVE **GOTHAM CITY**...

THAT LOOKS LIKE THE **AURORA BOREALIS**!

STRANGE-- IT USUALLY APPEARS FAR NORTH OF HERE-- IT'S HARDLY EVER SEEN IN **GOTHAM CITY**!

SUDDENLY, THE BRILLIANT LIGHTS FADE, AND...

BATMAN-- TWO UMBRELLAS! THEY CAUSED THE MULTI-COLORED LIGHTS!

YES--NOW THE LIGHTS ARE GONE, AND THEY'RE COMING DOWN! ONE IS A "PARACHUTE" UMBRELLA-- AND THE ONE SUSPENDED FROM IT HAS A SPARKLER ON IT! WHAT'S UP?

RACING TO WHERE THE STRANGE PAIR OF UMBRELLAS LANDED...

I DON'T SEE ANY **OBVIOUS** GIMMICKS IN THE UMBRELLAS-- BUT LET'S TAKE A CLOSER LOOK! THE **PENGUIN** DOESN'T MAKE **ANYTHING** OBVIOUS!

8

THE RODS OF THIS ONE ARE HOLLOW--NOT GIMMICKED WITH ANYTHING, AS FAR AS I CAN SEE!

SAME WITH THIS ONE! BUT SOMEHOW I CAN'T BELIEVE THE PENGUIN WOULD DROP TWO MEANING-LESS UMBRELLAS!

ISN'T THAT KIND OF A LOUD COLOR DESIGN?

THE SAME IDEA STRUCK ME! YOU KNOW--MAYBE THE COLORS ARE A CLUE TO THE PENGUIN'S PLOTTING! HE'D LIKE TO TAUNT US BY THROWING A CLUE TO HIS UP-COMING CRIME AT US, JUST TO SEE IF WE COULD TUMBLE TO IT!

COULD BE THAT THE COLORS INDICATE THE KIND OF JOB HE HOPES TO PULL!

POSSIBLY--BUT IS IT ONE COLOR THAT'S IMPORTANT, OR ALL OF THEM? THE GREEN COULD BE FOR EMERALDS--OR MONEY! YET, ALL THE COLORS TOGETHER COULD MEAN A COLLECTION OF GEMS!

HOLD IT! "COLLECTION OF GEMS"! THE MOST VALUABLE COLLECTION IN TOWN IS THE JEWELED METEORITE ON DISPLAY AT THE MUSEUM! IT'S STUDDED WITH EMERALDS, DIAMONDS, RUBIES--

AND THEIR COLORS MATCH THE UMBRELLA'S COLORS!

BUT EVEN AS BATMAN AND ROBIN VOICE THEIR DEDUCTIONS--

THAT MUST BE IT, BATMAN! THE PENGUIN'S PLANNING TO STEAL THE JEWELED METEORITE!

HA! I TOLD YOU I'M AS WISE AS AN OWL! OUR TWO FRIENDS DON'T REALIZE THEY'RE TALKING INTO A TINY TRANSISTOR MICRO-PHONE, CONCEALED IN THE "PARACHUTE" UMBRELLA!

ONE HALF OF MY PREDICTION HAS COME TRUE-- BATMAN HAS TOLD ME WHAT TO STEAL! NEXT, HE'LL TELL ME HOW TO DO IT! LISTEN...

BUT THE *PENGUIN* WILL HAVE HIS TROUBLES, *BATMAN!* THE METEORITE IS ON DISPLAY BEHIND A *BREAKPROOF* WINDOW--

AND GUARDS ARE CONSTANTLY ON DUTY IN THE ROOMS FLANKING THE DISPLAY ROOM, AS WELL AS IN THE CORRIDORS! *BUT--* THERE'S ONE WEAK SPOT...

...THE *ROOF!* THE *PENGUIN* COULD LAND ON THE ROOF BY PARACHUTE-UMBRELLA, AND THEN....

"AFTER LANDING, HIS GANG COULD CUT THROUGH THE ROOM WITH AN ACETYLENE TORCH...."

"AND BY USING A TRICK UMBRELLA WITH AN *EXTENSION* CANE, HE COULD REACH FAR DOWN, HOOK THE JEWELED METEORITE...."

--AND BE OFF WITH HIS PRIZE BEFORE THE GUARDS KNEW WHAT HAPPENED!

SEE! *BATMAN* NOT ONLY SELECTED MY CRIME, BUT *BLUE-PRINTED* IT FOR ME! I'LL USE HIS PLAN-- BUT WITH MY *OWN* SPECIAL TOUCH!

LET'S GO! THE *PENGUIN* WILL STRIKE...RIGHT BEFORE *BATMAN'S* EYES, WHERE HE'LL BE WAITING ON THE ROOF! DON'T FORGET THE *PENGUIN-MAGNET*, HERBIE!

GOT IT, BOSS!

10

WE WERE ABLE TO TURN ON MY **P-MAGNET** AT ANY TIME, DRAWING YOU TO IT! IT'S INSIDE THE ELEVATOR SHED ACROSS YONDER ROOF!

THAT PESKY **PENGUIN**-- ONE STEP AHEAD OF US AGAIN!

STUCK--LIKE FLIES IN FLYPAPER!

JUST AS WE DEDUCED, THE **PENGUIN'S** USED AN ACETYLENE TORCH TO CUT THROUGH THE ROOF, AND MUST BE PULLING THE JEWELED METEORITE OUT BY NOW! WE'VE **GOT** TO GET LOOSE-- BUT NOT WITH THOSE TWO WATCHING US LIKE HAWKS!

HEY--LOOK WHAT THE **PENGUIN'S** UP TO NOW!

I CAUGHT **BATMAN'S** SIGNAL! WHILE THOSE TWO CROOKS ARE DIS-TRACTED--WE'LL PULL TINY KNIVES FROM OUR BELTS--CUT THE BELTS LOOSE, AND,...

HUH?

WITHIN MOMENTS, **BATMAN** AND **ROBIN** HAVE FREED THEMSELVES AND SLAMMED INTO THE TWO CROOKS...

WE'LL COOL OFF THESE TWO, **ROBIN**--THEN GET OUR **BATROPES** FROM THE BELTS AND RUFFLE THE **PENGUIN'S** FEATHERS!

12

THEN, AS THEY SWING TOWARD THE MUSEUM ROOF...

THE *PENGUIN'S* GOT THE METEORITE--AND IS ESCAPING WITH A *JET*-UMBRELLA!

GO AHEAD, BOSS-- WE'LL HOLD OFF *BATMAN* AN' THE KID!

BUT TO THE ASTONISHMENT OF THE CROOKS...

THIS **RING-AROUND-THE ROSY** TRICK SHOULD KEEP 'EM IN KNOTS FOR AWHILE, EH?

YES--YOU MIGHT SAY THEY'D LIKE TO GO SOMEWHERE-- BUT THEY'RE ALL *"TIED UP"*!

WITH THE LAST OF THE CROOKS TRUSSED UP...

IT SEEMS THERE'S NO WAY FOR US TO GO AFTER THE *PENGUIN*-- TILL YOU **WONDER** HOW THE TWO CROOKS WITH HIM WERE GOING TO GET AWAY...

OF COURSE! THEIR UMBRELLAS MUST *ALSO* BE JET-EQUIPPED!

AND THEN BEGINS AN ASTONISHING CHASE THROUGH NIGHT SKIES...

FROM NOW ON IT'S A QUESTION OF WHICH JET-UMBRELLA IS THE FASTEST--THE *PENGUIN'S*... OR ONE OF OURS!

DRAT IT! *ROBIN'S* PULLED AHEAD OF *BATMAN*--AND IS GAINING ON ME! IT'S A QUESTION OF WEIGHT! THE METEORITE IS SLOWING ME DOWN! ESCAPE IS THE MAIN ISSUE, SO...

13

HE JETTISONED THE METEORITE! I'LL GO AFTER IT, ROBIN! YOU STICK WITH THE PENGUIN!

HE'S STARTING TO PICK UP SPEED! BUT I KNOW HOW TO OVERCOME THAT...

ROBIN'S ROPE WHISTLES THROUGH THE AIR, AND...

SNARED HIM!

eh? WHAT'S THIS?

SOON...

LIKE A HOMING PIGEON, YOU'RE FLYING BACK TO WHERE YOU BELONG... A CAGE IN JAIL!

BAH!

LATER, AFTER THE JEWELED METEORITE IS RETRIEVED...

THE CASE IS BEATEN, PENGUIN-- EXCEPT FOR THE MYSTERY OF WHY YOU PULLED THE MONOCLE SWITCH! WE'RE TAKING IT ALONG FOR FURTHER STUDY!

HA! LET 'EM BAT THEIR BRAINS OUT! THEY'LL NEVER SOLVE THAT PART OF THE CASE.. WHICH GIVES THIS OLD BIRD SOMEWHAT OF A VICTORY!

The End

14

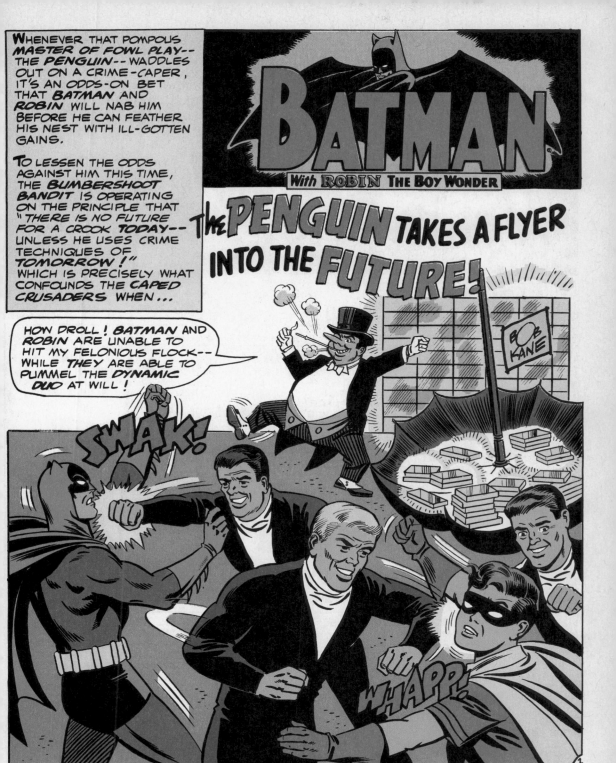

WHENEVER THAT POMPOUS *MASTER OF FOWL PLAY*-- THE *PENGUIN*--WADDLES OUT ON A CRIME-CAPER, IT'S AN ODDS-ON BET THAT *BATMAN* AND *ROBIN* WILL NAB HIM BEFORE HE CAN FEATHER HIS NEST WITH ILL-GOTTEN GAINS.

TO LESSEN THE ODDS AGAINST HIM THIS TIME, THE *BUMBERSHOOT BANDIT* IS OPERATING ON THE PRINCIPLE THAT "*THERE IS NO FUTURE FOR A CROOK TODAY*-- UNLESS HE USES CRIME TECHNIQUES OF *TOMORROW!*" WHICH IS PRECISELY WHAT CONFOUNDS THE *CAPED CRUSADERS* WHEN...

BATMAN
With ROBIN The Boy Wonder

The PENGUIN TAKES A FLYER INTO THE FUTURE!

HOW DROLL! *BATMAN* AND *ROBIN* ARE UNABLE TO HIT MY FELONIOUS FLOCK-- WHILE *THEY* ARE ABLE TO PUMMEL THE *DYNAMIC DUO* AT WILL!

BOB KANE

SWAK!

WHAPP!

Written by Gardner Fox/Art by Chic Stone & Sid Greene

FELLOW BIRD-BRAINS--MEET *CHEF PENGUIN*!

B-BUT, B-BOSS--YOU DIDN'T TELL US YOU HAD A TWIN BROTHER!

BOSH! WHAT YOU ARE SEEING IS MERELY A *ROBOT PENGUIN*! I'VE PROGRAMMED HIM TO BE THE WORLD'S GREATEST CHEF! AND HERE IS HIS CULINARY MASTERPIECE!

HUH? A BUNCH O' PILLS?

WHERE'S THE FOOD?

EGAD, YOU INDIGENT IGNORAMUSES! THESE PILLS *ARE* THE MEAL-- ONE FOR EACH OF US! WHAT YOU ARE ABOUT TO DINE UPON IS THE FEAST OF THE FUTURE!

EACH OF THESE PILLS CONTAINS ALL THE CONCENTRATED FOOD ELEMENTS OF A *CHATEAUBRIAND STEAK*--*CAESAR'S SALAD*--*POTATO AND VEGETABLES*-- AND *BAKED ALASKA*!

COME, COME-- EAT HEARTY, MY FINE-- FEATHERED FINKS! ENJOY THE FUTURE TODAY! WE HAVE A JOB TO DO THIS NIGHT!

I'D STILL RATHER DIG INTO A STEAK! BUT WHAT'S ALL THIS TALK ABOUT THE *FUTURE* YOU'RE SPOUTING?

I THOUGHT YOU'D NEVER ASK! YOU SEE BEFORE YOU A GENIUS WHO HAS COME TO GRIPS WITH THE FUTURE-- AND OUT-THOUGHT IT! BY JOVE! I--THE *PENGUIN*, MASTER OF FOWL PLAY, HAVE AT LAST COME INTO MY OWN!

TOO LONG HAVE WE PERMITTED THE LAW ENFORCEMENT AGENCIES OF OUR WORLD TO THWART US WITH THEIR SCIENTIFIC CRIME—DETECTION DEVICES! TODAY'S OUTDATED CROOK DOESN'T STAND A CHANCE! I HAVE DONE NOTHING IN ANSWER TO THIS CHALLENGE-- UNTIL NOW!

I HAVE NOT SHIRKED MY DUTY TO MY BROTHERS IN BANDITRY! THE PENGUIN HAS TURNED INTO THE DOVE OF THE ARK LEADING ALL OTHERS TO FOLLOW HIS EXAMPLE! YOUR AIR-CONDITIONED UNIFORMS AND INSTANT-ENERGY PILLS ARE JUST A SAMPLE OF HOW I HAVE UPDATED MY CRIME TECHNIQUES!

CHOMP!

CHOMP!

THIS VERY NIGHT--IF LUCK IS WITH US-- WE SHALL AGAIN TANGLE WITH BATMAN AND ROBIN! BUT THEY SHALL NOT CONFRONT BUMBLING BRAGGARTS AND HAPLESS HOODS! ON THE CONTRARY, THEY WILL FIND US INVENTIVE AND INGENIOUS!

WE SHALL BE INVIGORATED-- INCOMPARABLE--INVULNERABLE! THE DYNAMIC DUO SHALL GO DOWN BEFORE US LIKE PINS TO A BOWLING BALL IN THE HANDS OF AN EXPERT!

YA HEAR THAT, BALD EAGLE? THAT'S US TH' BOSS IS TALKIN' ABOUT!

THROUGH THE SWELTERING HEAT OF THE CITY STREETS COMES THE BATMOBILE THIS SAME NIGHT...

¡WHEWWWW! IT'S SO HOT I JUST SAW A DOG CHASING A CAT AND THEY WERE BOTH WALKING!

SPEAKING OF HEAT, ROBIN-- THE SONAR-OSCILLATOR SEEMS TO BE AFFECTED BY IT TOO!

WOW! FROM THE PATTERN OF THE SQUIGGLES, I'D SAY SOME CROOK IS WORKING A NUCLEAR-POWERED DRILL! BUT WHAT CROOK COULD WHIP UP A GIMMICK LIKE THAT?

LET'S GO FIND OUT, ROBIN!

INTO THE OFFICES OF THE INTERNATIONAL GOLD CORPORATION RACE THE MASKED MANHUNTER AND BOY WONDER...

THERE'S OUR ANSWER, **BATMAN**-- THAT WISE OLD BIRD THE *PENGUIN!*

AH! MY FOOTLOOSE AND FANCY-FREE FOES! *HALT!* YOU'VE GONE *FAR* ENOUGH!

NEXT INSTANT...

HUH-- WHAT'S THIS? MY FEET FEEL SO HEAVY--I CAN'T EVEN MOVE THEM!

¡YUK! ¡YUK! YOU'VE BEEN CAUGHT FLAT-FOOTED BY MY HEAVY *GRAVITY BEAM!*

A *GRAVITY BEAM?* BUT NOBODY'S EVER INVENTED SUCH A-- *OOFF!*

HOW DROLL! YOU CAN HARDLY MOVE-- YET YOU DENY THE TRUTH OF WHAT'S HAPPENING TO YOU! HIT HIM AGAIN, *SWIFTY!*

TH WOKK!

I'M SO HEAVY-FOOTED HE KEEPS BEATING ME TO THE PUNCH!

THUMP!

ROBIN, TOO, FINDS HIMSELF DESPERATELY HANDICAPPED BY THE FUTURISTIC DEVICE OF THE *BUMBERSHOOT BANDIT...*

DIDN'T HOLD HIM, *ROBIN* WOULD BE FLYIN' CLEAR ACROSS THE ROOM!

SWOK!

5

93

OOF--CAN'T GET CLOSE ENOUGH TO LAY A HAND ON HIM!

HA, HA! THAT OL' GRAVITY BEAM'S GOT YA, ROBIN! YUH'RE SLOWER'N MOLASSES!

I WONDER WHY THE PENGUIN'S GANG IS NOT AFFECTED BY THE GRAVITY BEAM-- THE WAY WE ARE! COULD IT BE BECAUSE--

AS WE RAN IN-- WE POUNDED OVER SOMETHING THAT GRATED UNDER OUR BOOTS! IF THOSE WERE IRON FILLINGS--

ROBIN-- QUICKLY! GET OUT OF YOUR BOOTS! THE PENGUIN MUST HAVE CONCEALED A POWERFUL ELECTRIC MAGNET UNDER THE FLOOR --

JUST WHAT I WAS THINKING! THE MAGNETISM'S GRIPPING THE IRON FILINGS STUCK TO OUR BOOT SOLES AND HOLDING US TIGHT-- JUST AS A REAL GRAVITY BEAM MIGHT DO!

WITHOUT OUR BOOTS -- WE'RE OUR FIGHTING SELVES AGAIN!

TH-WUKK!

NOW IT'S OUR TURN TO DISH OUT THE SOKS AND POWS!

SSWOOSH

EGAD! THOSE TWO HAVE THE CALCULATING MINDS OF A COUPLE OF COMPUTERS!

6

7

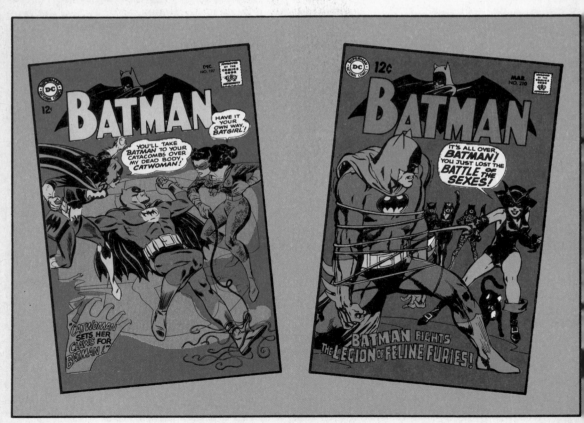

The PENGUIN TAKES A FLYER -- INTO THE FUTURE!

PART 2

SWEPT OFF THEIR FEET BY THE UNEXPECTED ONSLAUGHT, *BATMAN* AND *ROBIN* RECOVER SWIFTLY-- SEND FLYING FISTS AT THEIR FOES...

HERE I GO AGAIN-- WITH A SECOND HELPING OF PUNCH PUDDING!

THOSE CROOKS MUST BE SO STUNNED AT OUR OWN RAPID RECOVERY, THEY'RE NOT EVEN MAKING A MOVE TO STOP US!

WHY SHOULD THEY? THEY KNOW YOU CAN'T LAY A HAND ON THEM!

M-MISSED HIM! WHA--?

MY FIST SWERVED OFF-COURSE!

HOW COULD I MISS SUCH AN EASY TARGET? I'LL TRY IT AGAIN--

HAW! HAW! YOU COULDN'T HIT THE SIDE OF A BARN, *BATMAN!*

AND ONCE AGAIN HIS ARM SWINGS WILDLY...

WATCH CLOSELY, *BATMAN*-- I'LL SHOW YOU HOW IT'S DONE!

9

WHILE *BATMAN'S* FISTS KEEP MISSING, HIS WITS KEEP CLICKING...

FOR ALL *PENGUIN'S* BOASTS, I CAN'T BELIEVE HE'S COME UP WITH A "FIST-FENDER-OFF"! IT'S GOT TO BE A TRICK--TO MAKE IT APPEAR THAT WAY!

SOCK!

ROBIN, TOO, IS ALERT TO WHAT GOES ON AROUND HIM...

MAYBE I'M *TELE-GRAPHING MY PUNCHES*! THAT WOULD MEAN THE MAN I'M FIGHTING KNOWS *WHERE* I'M GOING TO HIT! BUT SUPPOSE I *FAKE* A PUNCH? I'LL FEINT A *RIGHT* AND STRIKE FAST WITH MY *LEFT*...

ZOK!

THE *DYNAMIC DUO* ACTS AS ONE...

THE CROOK THINKS I'M GOING TO HIT HIM WITH A RIGHT FIST BUT ...

...I'LL SOCK HIM WITH A LIGHTNING LEFT JAB!

ZWUPP!

THWAKK!

AS HE FOLLOWS THROUGH, *BAT-MAN'S* CHEEK COMES CLOSE TO THE BANDIT'S UNIFORM AND...

SO THAT'S IT! THEIR UNIFORMS ARE EQUIPPED TO RELEASE AIR UNDER HIGH PRESSURE AT CERTAIN POINTS! WHEN THE CROOK SEES WHERE MY PUNCH IS AIMED, HE SENDS OUT A CONCENTRATED BLAST OF AIR TO HIT MY FIST AND BRUSH IT ASIDE!

KRAK!

11

NOW THAT WE'VE SOLVED THE SECRET OF THEIR "INVULNERABILITY"...

SOK!

...WE MISS WITH ONE-- AND CONNECT WITH THE OTHER!

THWAKK!

AS THE LAST OF HIS CROOKED FLOCK IS GROUNDED, THE BUMBERSHOOT BUCCANEER WADDLES OFF...

BOPP!

WHUKK!!

ODZOOKS! CAN NOTHING STOP THOSE FLYING FISTED DO-GOODERS?

WE'RE TOO LATE! THERE HE GOES ON HIS JET-- UMBRELLA!

YES, BOY WONDER! IT'S TIME I FLEW THIS CON-FOUNDED "COUP"...WITH ALL THE GOLD I CAN CARRY IN MY UMBRELLA CANOPY!

AS HE RACES ACROSS THE NIGHT SKY, BITTER REALIZATION COMES TO THE PENGUIN...

MY BIRD-BRAIN GANG WAS INCAPABLE OF THINKING AS FAST AS BATMAN AND ROBIN! I'LL HAVE TO DEVISE SOME NEW MEANS OF HANDLING THOSE TWO!

SHORTLY, IN HIS SUBTERRANEAN NEST...

AH--YES! I HAVE IT! JUST AS I CREATED A *ROBOT PENGUIN*, I SHALL MAKE ROBOT UMBRELLAS--*ROBOTRELLAS*--TO STEAL AND DO BATTLE FOR ME!

BY CONTROLLING THEIR EVERY MOVE WITH MY OWN BRAIN, I WILL BE IN COMPLETE COMMAND AT ALL TIMES! NOW--TO WORK, TO WORK!

BACK IN *GOTHAM CITY*, AFTER THEY HAVE TAKEN THEIR PRISONERS TO JAIL, THE *DYNAMIC DUO* HEADS HOMEWARD...

PENGUIN SURE TOOK A FLYER--INTO THE FUTURE! I WONDER WHAT STUNTS HE'LL WHIP UP FOR US NEXT TIME WE MEET?

NO ONE KNOWS WHAT TOMORROW WILL BRING, *ROBIN!* WE MUST BE ON GUARD AT ALL TIMES!

SOME NIGHTS LATER, SILENT SHAPES JET SMOOTHLY THROUGH THE AIR...

MUFFLERS PREVENT MY *ROBBER-ROBOTRELLAS* FROM MAKING ANY NOISE!

TINY *LASER BEAMS* MELT THE GLASS WINDOWS WITHOUT SETTING OFF THE BURGLAR ALARMS, PERMITTING MY *BUMBER-SHOOT BANDITS* TO ENTER!

FROM HIS UNDERGROUND NEST, THE *PENGUIN* GLOATS AS...

AFTER USING CONCEALED MAGNETS IN THEIR HANDLES TO OPEN SAFE DOORS, I REMOTE-CONTROL MY *PLUNDERING PARASOLS* TO CHOOSE MY LOOT FOR ME!

13

BY SCANNING EACH JEWEL WITH A JEWELER'S EYE-PIECE, THEY WILL SELECT ONLY THE FINEST STONES FOR MY ENJOYMENT!

BUT AS THOSE BANDIT BUMBERSHOOTS GIVE OFF ELECTRONIC SIGNALS WHILE THEY FUNCTION ...

BATMAN! WE'RE IN TUNE WITH ELECTRONIC IMPULSES! THEY SOUND LIKE SOUR NOTES TO ME!

THEY'RE COMING FROM THAT JEWELRY STORE!

BATMAN-- LOOK! JET-UMBRELLAS--

--WHICH SPELL OUT PENGUIN! BUT WHERE'S THE EMPEROR BIRD?

NO SIGN OF OUR MAN OF A THOUSAND UMBRELLAS! HE MUST BE ROBOT-CONTROLLING THEM FROM HIS HIDE-OUT!

FRAMED IN THEIR BAT-NOCULARS THEY SEE A CARAVAN OF WEALTH AS THE JEWELS GLOW WITH INCANDESCENT COLORS...

INTO THE BATMOBILE, ROBIN! THOSE UMBRELLAS WILL LEAD US TO OUR PREY!

FOR A COUPLE OF MINUTES THEY KEEP THE ROBOTRELLAS IN SIGHT UNTIL ...

THEY'RE GETTING OUT OF RANGE-- MOVING FASTER AND FASTER!

LOOKS LIKE THE PENGUIN'S GETTING AWAY WITH HIS SKYWAY ROBBERY!

14

JUST FOR *THIS* TIME, *ROBIN*! WHEN HE STRIKES AGAIN, WE'LL HAVE THE SCIENTIFIC SOLUTION TO HIS ROBBERIES-BY-UMBRELLAS-- *BAT-RELLAS*!

WE'LL BEAT HIM AT HIS OWN GAME, EH?

SOON COWLED CRU-SADER AND *BOY WONDER* ARE HARD AT WORK IN THE *BAT-CAVE...*

WHERE CAN *ALFRED* BE? I SENT HIM FOR THOSE SPECIAL TRANSISTORS WE NEED FOR THIS JOB!

THE CONCEALED *BAT-DOOR* OPENS -- AND A GUST OF WIND USHERS ALFRED THE BUTLER AND A SPRAY OF RAIN INTO THE *BATCAVE...*

HERE I AM, SIR! I DIDN'T WANT TO AROUSE AUNT HARRIET'S SUSPICIONS, SO I CAME IN BY THE HILLSIDE ENTRANCE!

WHAT A TERRIBLE NIGHT IT IS! A GOOD THING I HAD MY TRUSTY UMBRELLA ALONG!

SAY-- THAT BUMBERSHOOT OF YOURS GIVES ME AN IDEA, ALFRED! YOU MAY COME IN USEFUL IN OUR NEXT TRY FOR THE *PENGUIN*!

FAR FROM THE *BAT-CAVE*, ELATION SURGES THROUGH THE POUTER-PIGEON CHEST OF THE *BIRDMAN BANDIT* AS HE HOLDS UP A HANDFUL OF HIS LOOT..

EGAD! I'M A GENIUS'S GENIUS! MY *ROBOTRELLAS* ARE THE PERFECT THIEVES!

HEIGH-HO! ORDINARILY I WOULD NEVER REPEAT THE SAME METHOD OF COMMITTING A CRIME -- BUT THIS METHOD IS SO SPECTACULAR, SO SAFE, THAT I SHALL MAKE AN EXCEPTION IN THIS CASE -- FOR THE *DYNAMIC DUO'S* BENEFIT!

MANY MILES OUTSIDE **GOTHAM CITY** THE **ROBOTRELLAS** DROP DOWN ONTO AN EMPTY FIELD...

THE ROBOT UMBRELLAS ARE GETTING RID OF THEIR LOOT!

WHERE HIS LOOT IS, CAN THE **PENGUIN** BE FAR BEHIND?

IN HIS UNDERGROUND HIDEAWAY, THE **BUMBERSHOOT BUCCANEER** GLOATS WITH EVIL SATISFACTION...

NO, **BATMAN!** I AM CLOSE BY, READY TO TURN MY FIGHTING FORCES INTO-- **DYNAMIC DUO DEATH-DEALERS!**

AND THEN-- THEIR CANOPIES WHIRLING MADLY, APPEAR THE FIGHTING FORCES OF THE **MAN OF 1000 UMBRELLAS!**...

whoa! UMBRELLA ATTACK HEADED OUR WAY!

BRACE YOURSELF, **ROBIN!** THIS MAY BE THE TOUGHEST FIGHT OF OUR LIVES!

YEOW! TWO OF THEM TEAMING UP AGAINST ME!

USING THIS MACE-UMBRELLA-- TO PULL ME FREE OF THE NECK-GRABBING ONE!

17

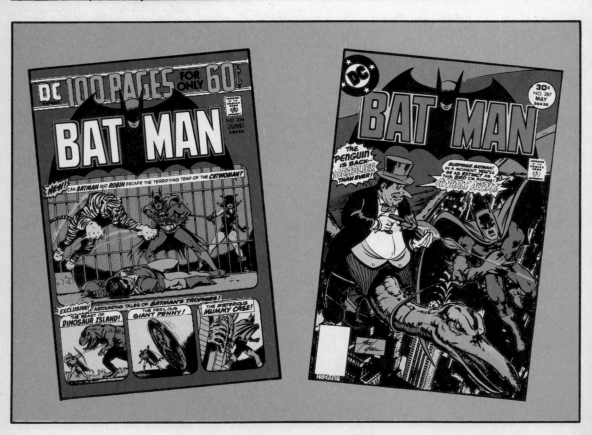

THE PENGUIN TAKES A FLYER--INTO THE FUTURE!
PART 3

SO INTENT ARE THEY ON THEIR DESPERATE STRUGGLE FOR SURVIVAL THAT THEY FAIL TO SEE TWO *NET-BRELLAS* SWOOPING DOWN ON THEM ...

I MANEUVERED THOSE THINGS INTO POSITION--AND DUCKED JUST IN TIME!

BY KNOCKING 'EM OFF TWO AT A TIME, THE *PENGUIN* WILL SOON RUN OUT OF UMBRELLAS!

THE FLYING *NET-BRELLAS* DROP DOWN-- CABLES LENGTHEN TO GATHER IN THEIR PREY...

YIII! THAT WAS A *NET* LOSS-- FOR US!

THAT'S IT, *ROBIN!* NO MATTER WHAT THE DANGER-- DON'T LOSE YOUR SENSE OF HUMOR!

TWISTED INSIDE THE NETTING OF METALLIC CABLES, THE TRAPPED DUO IS FLOWN TO THE *PENGUIN'S* NEST...

OH, HAPPY HOUR! OH, DELIGHTFUL DAY! YOU ARE MY PRISONERS AT LAST, *BATMAN* AND *ROBIN!* NOW YOU SHALL PAY THE PENALTY LONG OVERDUE YOU!

THE GAME'S NOT OVER TILL THE LAST OUT, *PENGUIN*--AND THAT'S WHAT WE'LL DO NEXT-- GET *OUT!*

GRIPPING THE NET STRANDS, THE TERRIFIC TWOSOME SWINGS THEM TOGETHER SO THAT THE UM- BRELLAS ARE DRIVEN FOR- WARD INTO THE *WICKED WADDLER!*..

THIS WILL LOOSEN THE NETS JUST ENOUGH FOR *ROBIN* AND MY- SELF TO FREE OUR- SELVES OF THIS GRIP!

20

SURRENDER, *PENGUIN*!

WE'VE GOT A JAIL-CAGE ALL READY FOR YOU!

TUT-TUT! DID YOU FORGET I AM MASTER OF THE FUTURE? OBSERVE--!

HUH? THE *PENGUIN*-- FLYING!?

NOT EVEN A *REAL* PENGUIN— BIRD CAN DO THAT!

A DEMONSTRATION OF MY MIND-OVER-MATTER CONTROL OF OBJECTS SHOULD CONVINCE YOU OF THE FUTILITY OF RESISTING ME!

HURLING FURNITURE AT US?!

ACTING WITH INSTANTANEOUS TEAMWORK--THE *DYNAMIC DUO* GRIPS CHAIR-ARMS AND TABLE-LEGS AND...

AS *CHAIR-MAN* I VOTE THAT WE *TABLE* THIS DISCUSSION UNTIL *PENGUIN* TAKES THE *FLOOR*, BATMAN!

I *TOLD* YOU I HAD MASTERED GRAVITY! I AM NO LONGER EARTH-BOUND! NOW *YOU* SURRENDER TO ME BEFORE I USE MY FUTURISTIC ABILITIES TO DESTROY YOU BOTH!

AS THE THROWN CHAIR AND TABLE THUD INTO THE CEILING-HIGH *PENGUIN*...

HOLY DECEPTION! THAT'S A *ROBOT* PENGUIN!

BARROOM!

WE'VE BEEN TRICKED AGAIN, *ROBIN*!

21

As we knew, **Penguin** had no gravity control -- nor mind-over-matter ability! He worked those tricks by cunningly planted magnets!

The **real Penguin** was out of our reach all the time! I wonder where he is?

But search as they will, the **caped crime-fighters** cannot locate their quarry! Finally, when they glumly return to the **batmobile**...

Alfred! **You** caught the **Penguin!**

Your trick of using Alfred paid off, **Batman!**

Indeed it did, **Master Robin!** When you left me hidden in the **Batmobile** trunk and I saw you netted and carried off -- I almost gave chase -- but you had told me to watch the loot -- so in due time when I saw the ground opening and the loot dropped down into it I leaped after it!

"**I** rained down on the **Penguin** along with his stolen money..."

Egad! What's this? I've caught a butler along with my bank notes...

"Before the fowl bandit could move against me, I bashed him with my trusty umbrella..."

That will lay you out while I take you and your ill-gotten gains to the **Batmobile!**

Evidently he had two underground hide-outs! One from which he controlled his umbrellas and his robot other self, the other where he had us brought!

I imagine he equipped his robots with television cameras to see and hear what was going on -- so he could utilize them most effectively! Well, **Penguin's** flyer has led him back to prison!

22

SOMEWHAT LATER, IN THE *BUMBERSHOOT BANDIT'S* CELL...

YOU WON'T HANDLE AN UMBRELLA FOR A LONG WHILE IN THERE, *PENGUIN!*

ARE *YOU* THE *PENGUIN?* IT'S A GREAT HONOR TO BE YOUR CELL MATE!

INDEED, MY GOOD MAN? YES, I RATHER IMAGINE IT IS! WHAT IS YOUR NAME!

BROLLY--

BROLLY!? WHY--THAT'S THE ENGLISH SLANG WORD FOR AN *UMBRELLA!*

SO *BATMAN* AND *ROBIN* THINK I CAN'T COME IN CONTACT WITH AN "UMBRELLA" IN HERE, DO THEY? WELL--THIS *BROLLY* CHARACTER IS AN "UMBRELLA" THAT WILL PROVE OF INESTIMABLE AID IN ENABLING ME TO ESCAPE FROM THIS NEFARIOUS NEST OF PENAL SERVITUDE!

The End /23

WHAT A DESIGNING WOMAN WAS—*CATWOMAN!* SHE HAD DESIGNS ON SNARING *BATMAN* FOR HER MATE—EVEN IF IT MEANT ABANDONING HER ROLE AS THE *PRINCESS OF PLUNDER!* IF THE WORST CAME TO PASS AND HE TURNED HER DOWN, SHE'D MANAGE TO SURVIVE WITHOUT *BATMAN*—WHILE MAKING SURE *HE* DIDN'T LIVE AT ALL!

"*CATWOMAN Sets Her Claws for BATMAN!*"

I CAN'T FIGURE OUT WHETHER SHE'S TRYING TO SHOW *US* UP -- OR *BATGIRL* --

-- OR *BOTH!*

AT LEAST SHE'S "REFORMED" IN ONE WAY! IN THE PAST, HER CRIMINAL ACTIVITIES USED TO INVOLVE A "CAT" IN SOME WAY OR OTHER! BUT THERE'S NO "CAT" IN *GOTHAM WINERY!*

NOT SO, *ROBIN!* I HAPPEN TO KNOW THE *GOTHAM WINERY* USES *CATAWBA* GRAPES TO MAKE ITS WINES!

SO MAYBE SHE *DOES* HAVE A CAT-TRICK HIDDEN BEHIND HER CAT-MASK! WE'LL JUST HAVE TO POSSESS THE PATIENCE OF A CAT -- TO LEARN WHAT IT IS!

THE FOLLOWING NIGHT THE *BAT-MOBILE'S* DETECTION GEAR LOCATES A ROBBERY AT A SILK HANDKERCHIEF FACTORY...

NO SIGN OF OUR RIVAL -- OR *BATGIRL!*

THAT SUITS ME FINE! NABBING CROOKS IS *MAN'S* WORK!

SILK FACTORY LTD.

AS IF TO REDEEM THEMSELVES IN THEIR OWN EYES (AFTER ALL, *CATWOMAN* CAUGHT THE PARKER GANG), THE *CAPED CRUSADER* AND *BOY WONDER* HURL THEMSELVES INTO THE FRAY...

A *NECK-LOCK HIP-THROW* FOR THIS ONE --

-- AND AN OLD-FASHIONED *BELT* IN THE STOMACH FOR MY CUSTOMER!

THAT WRAPS UP THIS TWO-SOME!

TOO BAD THERE AREN'T MORE! I'VE JUST BEGUN TO FIGHT!

5

118

SUDDENLY OUT OF THE SHADOWS OF THE HANDKER-CHIEF FACTORY, WHIPS THE *BATROPE*...

THAT WAS GOOD *NOOSE,* BATMAN...

SOON AS I CLEAR MY HEAD-- I'LL PITCH IN...

BUT AS THE *MASKED MAN-HUNTER* HAULS IN HIS CATCH...

THEY-- RUSHED ME--!

NEXT MOMENT SIX GUNS LIFT AS SIX FINGERS CURL ABOUT HALF A DOZEN TRIGGERS...

OBVIOUSLY, *BATMAN* AND *ROBIN* CAN USE A HELPING HAND!

INCHES FROM THE EARS OF THE SEXTET OF GUNMEN, TINY BOMBS ATTACHED TO THE THONGS OF THE *CAT-O-NINE TAILS* DETONATE WITH DEAFENING FURY...

BOOM!

CRACK!

BLAPP!

BLAM!

WHOPP!

EEEEY! IT'S LIKE MY HEAD WAS BUSTIN' OPEN!

CRACK!

QUICK, *ROBIN*-- BEFORE THEY RE-COVER FROM THAT NOISE BOMBARDMENT!

FOR ONCE IN MY LIFE--I'M ACTUALLY HAPPY TO SEE YOU, *CATWOMAN!*

8

IF YOU WANT A FELINE FRIEND TO HELP YOU PLAY CAT-AND-MOUSE WITH ANY MORE ROBBERS-- *REMEMBER CATWOMAN!*

YOU DEFINITELY ARE IN NEED OF -- A WOMAN'S TOUCH!

WHY IS SHE MAKING THOSE *CATTY REMARKS* ABOUT *BATGIRL?*

AS THE *FELINE FURY* DRIVES OFF...

ONE THING'S FOR SURE-- WE COULDN'T HAVE DONE AS WELL AS WE DID WITHOUT HER!

THERE'S NOTHING ABOUT A "CAT" IN A SILK HANDKERCHIEF FACTORY! PERHAPS SHE'S REFORMED PERMANENTLY!

HAS *CATWOMAN* REALLY ABANDONED HER CAT-MOTIVE? THIS BURNING THOUGHT SEARS THE MIND OF BARBARA (*BATGIRL*) GORDON NEXT DAY IN THE LIBRARY OF WHICH SHE IS BOSS-LADY...

I SEEM TO REMEMBER SOMETHING ABOUT SILK HANDKERCHIEFS...A PARTICULAR WORD THAT MY PHOTOGRAPHIC MEMORY TELLS ME MAY FIT IN...

ALONE IN HER OFFICE, SHE TURNS ON THE RADIO, FOR BABS GORDON HAS TRAINED HERSELF TO READ A BOOK AND SIMULTANEOUSLY ABSORB WHAT IS BEING SAID TO HER...

IF *ROBIN* COULD SEE ME NOW, HE'D SAY THAT SINCE I HAVE A *PHOTOGRAPHIC MEMORY*, I OUGHT TO WEAR A *FILM*Y DRESS WHEN I USE IT...

CLICK

⑩

OUR REPORTER ON THE SPOT INFORMS US THAT LAST NIGHT WHEN *BATMAN* MADE HIS REPORT TO THE POLICE, HE TOLD THEM THAT *CATWOMAN* AGAIN REMARKED -- "ANYTHING BATGIRL CAN DO, *I* CAN DO -- *BETTER!*"

AH -- HERE'S THAT WORD --

PULICAT!

Pulicat

A *PULICAT* IS A SILK BANDANA OR HANDKERCHIEF! IT DERIVES ITS NAME FROM *LAKE PULICAT* IN *MADRAS, INDIA*, WHERE IT IS MANUFACTURED -- WHAT'S THAT?

CATWOMAN MENTIONING *BATGIRL?*

THE INFERENCE WAS THAT CATWOMAN WAS MOCKING BATGIRL...

WAS SHE NOW? MAYBE I'D JUST BETTER SEE FOR MYSELF, NEXT TIME SHE GOES PROWLING IN THAT KITTY CAR OF HERS!

SHE'S ROUSED MY FEMININE CURIOSITY-- AS WELL AS MY FEMININE INTUITION!

AND THAT SAME INTUITION TELLS ME CATWOMAN WILL STRIKE AT THE GOTHAM WAX MUSEUM-- WHERE A BIER OF A FAR EASTERN MAHARAJAH IS ON LOAN FROM HIS NATIVE COUNTRY!

ESPECIALLY SINCE A BIER IS ALSO KNOWN AS A-- CATAFALQUE!

THERE ARE TREASURE CHESTS OF REAL EMERALDS, REAL DIAMONDS, REAL PEARLS AT THAT CATAFALQUE, TO LEND THE WAX FIGURE AN AIR OF REALITY AS IT LIES IN STATE!

IF CROOKS MAKE A TRY FOR THOSE JEWELS-- CATWOMAN IS BOUND TO MAKE A TRY FOR THE CROOKS!

INSIDE HER PRIVATE CLOSET, FINGERS PULL DOWN THE ROLL-RIM OF A BERET, FORMING A COWL...

NEITHER OF THEM IS GOING TO GET WHAT THEY WANT...

...FOR A SHOWDOWN WITH CATWOMAN...

...BECAUSE I'M GOING TO SHOW UP...

REVERSING HER SKIRT, SHE TURNS IT INTO A CAPE...

SHE ROLLS UP HER BOOT-FLAPS...

HER SPECIALLY DESIGNED HANDBAG BECOMES HER WEAPONS-POUCH...

...AS BATGIRL!

THAT NIGHT SHE SPEEDS CROSSTOWN ON HER *BATBIKE*...

LET'S SEE WHAT CATWOMAN CAN DO-- THAT BATGIRL SUPPOSEDLY CAN'T DO-- *BETTER!*

AND SO-- WITHIN THE SHADOWS OF A *CATAFALQUE*...

WELL, WELL! IF IT ISN'T BATMAN'S UNPRECIOUS LITTLE HELP-MATE!

I'M HERE TO PREVENT CRIME, CATWOMAN-- WHAT'S *YOUR* EXCUSE?

12

WHEN CATWOMAN AND BATGIRL MEET--FEMALE TEMPERS ARE BOUND TO FLARE! WHAT EFFECT WILL THIS HAVE-- ON BATMAN HIMSELF?

AGAIN THE DOMINOED DAREDOLL IS OFF TARGET...

HURLED MYSELF AT HIS LEGS--

WHUMP!

AND ENDED UP AGAINST THIS CATAFALQUE POST?!

SUDDENLY THE CAT-O'-NINE TAILS LOOPS ACROSS THE ROOM...

THWAAK!

MUSTN'T HIT A LADY, BOYS-- ESPECIALLY WHEN SHE'S DOWN!

IN POLICE HEADQUARTERS, SOON AFTERWARD...

BATMAN! I'M GLAD YOU'RE HERE!

I'VE BEEN ASKING ALL ALONG IF BATGIRL COULD DO WHAT I COULD--AND NOW I HAVE THE PROOF POSITIVE!

GO ON, BATGIRL! TELL BATMAN WHAT HAPPENED!

REALLY! WHAT DID BATMAN EVER SEE IN YOU IN THE FIRST PLACE, BATGIRL?

YOU'VE MADE A MISHMASH OF THIS!

SHE'S RIGHT! I COULDN'T DO ANYTHING RIGHT--

BONK!

LET ME SHOW YOU HOW IT'S DONE, GIRLIE!

THE IDEA IS TO HIT THE CROOKS--LIKE SO!--AND KNOCK THEM OUT!

THEN ALL YOU HAVE TO DO IS TURN THEM OVER TO THE POLICE!

THWAK!

THE CRIME-PATROL BEGINS WITH THE *BATMOBILE* HEADING FOR A RARE COIN EMPORIUM! ALSO CONVERGING ON THAT SAME *COIN CHATEAU* ARE THE *KITTY CAR*-- AND THE *BATBIKE*...

THE COLLECTION OF *RARE DUCATS*--SILVER COINS ISSUED IN 1140 BY THE DUKE OF APULIA--MAY TEMPT SOME CROOKS INTO STRIKING FOR THEM!

STARTLED FACES LIFT FROM PILES OF COSTLY COINS AS...

BATMAN AND *ROBIN!*

WITH *CATWOMAN*--

AN' *BATGIRL* TOO!

WHAT ARE *YOU* DOING HERE, *BATGIRL?* I THOUGHT YOU'D LEARNED YOUR LESSON!

I THOUGHT I HAD, TOO-- UNTIL MY PHOTOGRAPHIC MEMORY RECALLED A CERTAIN WORD--

CATOPTRICS--THAT BRANCH OF OPTICS WHICH DEALS WITH THE REFLECTION OF LIGHT!

THE BAUBLE YOU KEPT SWINGING DISTORTED THE LIGHT-- AND MY VISION--JUST ENOUGH--TO THROW MY TIMING OFF!

TO HER INTENSE SURPRISE, THE *MASKED MAIDEN* DISCOVERS THAT *CATWOMAN* IS NOT EVEN LISTENING...

SINCE I KNEW *YOU'D* CAUSED ME TO LOOK BAD I DECIDED TO COME OUT TONIGHT! I GOT A FIX ON YOUR *KITTY CAR* AND--

SWOTT!

BATMAN-- LOOK OUT!

17

ONCE MORE THE *PRINCESS OF PLUNDER* STARES IN ANGRY DISMAY...

THEY'RE PAINT-MASKED TOO!

I'D TRY TO REMOVE THAT PAINT-- BUT IF THEY WERE ALL SO FORE-SIGHTED TO TAKE SUCH PRE-CAUTIONS, I'M SURE SOME SPECIAL CHEMICAL IS NEEDED TO GET RID OF IT!

PICK THEM UP! PUT THEM IN THE TRAP I'VE ARRANGED FOR THEM!

AND DON'T FORGET TO REMOVE THEIR UTILITY BELTS--AND WEAPONS-BAG!

SUMMONING HER MEN FROM THE NEXT ROOM, THE *FELINE FELON* SNAPS HER ORDERS...

SHORTLY...

GOOD! I SEE YOU CAME TO FIRST, *BATMAN!*

WE HAVE MATTERS TO TALK OVER, YOU AND I! YOU SEE, I REFORMED FOR YOU -- BUT YOU HAVEN'T REWARDED ME BY PROPOSING TO ME!

SO I'VE BROUGHT YOU HERE TO FORCE YOU TO DECIDE--

DO I GO BACK TO MY CRIME CAREER AS *CATWOMAN*--OR ARE YOU GOING TO SAY THE MAGIC WORDS "MARRY ME!"-- AND MAKE ME THE HAPPIEST GIRL IN THE WORLD?

NEITHER *ROBIN* NOR *BATGIRL* CAN HELP YOU NOW, SO DO I GO ON RUTHLESSLY ROBBING --OR ARE YOU GOING TO MAKE ME YOUR *BRIDE?*

I'VE HAD ENOUGH OF YOUR DILLY-DALLYING! MAKE UP YOUR MIND!

IT BEGINS THIS BRISK SPRING AFTERNOON AT THE CAMPUS OF *HUDSON UNIVERSITY...* WHERE *KING PEEBLE IV,* TWELVE-YEAR-OLD RULER OF THE KINGDOM OF *SWAWAK,* IS PAYING A VISIT...

YOUR *MAJESTY,* I'M *DICK GRAYSON!* THE COLLEGE PRESIDENT ASKED ME TO GIVE YOU THE *GRAND TOUR!*

YOU? A MERE *CHILD?* I *SHOULD* BE *INSULTED!*

I TRUST YOU ARE AT LEAST AN *HONOR STUDENT!*

FOR WHAT IT'S WORTH... I AM!

THIS IS A STATUE OF OUR *FOUNDER!* HE BUILT THE SCHOOL IN 1895 AND...

WHO *CARES?* I WANT TO SEE THE *"MALT SHOP"* WHERE THE *"CATS AND CHICKS HANG OUT"*-- JUST LIKE IN THE AMERICAN *FILMS!*

I AM INTERESTED IN *"SOCK HOPS"* AND *"BEACH BLANKET BIKINI BINGO"!*

ER... I'M AFRAID THE MOVIES GIVE A RATHER *DISTORTED* PICTURE OF OUR LIFE!

AS FOR BEACHES AND BIKINIS...IT'S A BIT EARLY IN THE *YEAR!*

BIT EARLY FOR SOMETHING *ELSE*--

--THOSE *BIRDS...* AND THEY'RE ACTING *STRANGELY!*

HOVERING OVER US... STARTING TO *SWOOP*--

--ATTACK!

2

136

I'M TAKING A *CHANCE*... SWITCHING IDENTITIES IN *BROAD DAYLIGHT*--

--BUT EVERYONE'S BUSY TRYING TO FEND OFF THOSE *WINGED NASTIES* --AND BESIDES, I NEED MY *CAPE* TO PROTECT MY *EYES!*

ODD... THEY'RE NOT GOING *NEAR* THE KING!

JUST GIVING THE MISERIES TO *EVERYONE ELSE!*

BRO-*THER!* IT'S LIKE FIGHTING A *FEATHERSTORM* FULL OF *BROKEN GLASS!*

CHUP.

CHUP.

HUH--? I HEAR AN *ENGINE*--

CHUP!

-- A *HELICOPTER*... LANDING AS THOUGH IT GOT A *CUE*-- WHICH I'M BETTING IT *DID!*

GOT TO GET THROUGH TO THE *KING!*

HE'S BEING *KIDNAPED!*

NO CHANCE OF REACHING HIM BEFORE THE 'COPTER *LEAVES*--

3

CHUP- CHUP- CHUP!

--BUT AT LEAST I CAN NAIL THIS SPECIMEN...

...HARD!

THE BATMAN WOULD SUBTLY THREATEN TO DISMEMBER HIM TO GET INFORMATION! ME, THOUGH, I'M A MORE PEACEFUL LAD!

TALK AND I MAY PUT IN A GOOD WORD AT YOUR TRIAL!

WHO'S YOUR BOSS?

YEAH-- I'LL TELL YA!

WHY NOT?

I SHOULD SUFFER FOR HIM?

A LARD-LEGGED DUDE NAMED FORSTER APTENODYTES PAID US TO PUT THE SNATCH ON THE SNOT!

HE ARRANGED THE GIMMICK WITH THE BIRDS--

--AND OTHER THAN THAT, I KNOW NOTHIN'! UNHH!

SOMEHOW, I FIND IT VERY EASY TO BELIEVE YOU!

TAKE HIM--HE'S YOURS!

HE'S GOING TO JAIL... AND I'M GOING TO GOTHAM CITY AS FAST AS MY CAMPER WILL CARRY ME!

...THE CITY--AND A CERTAIN CAVE--

4

SOON, *ROBIN* IS RELATING THE BIZARRE EVENTS TO HIS GUARDIAN AND MENTOR IN A HUGE CAVERN BENEATH A SUBURBAN MANSION...

THAT'S THE *STORY!* MAKE ANY *SENSE* TO YOU?

QUITE A *BIT!*

CONSIDER THE *METHOD* OF THE CRIME!

BIRDS, HIGHLY TRAINED *NOT* TO ATTACK THE *KING*--

--AND THE *NAME* THE HOOD GAVE YOU-- *FORSTER APTENODYTES!*

THE LABEL SCIENTISTS GIVE TO A CERTAIN BIRD IS--

--APTENODYTES FORSTERI...

...AND THAT BIRD IS THE *EMPEROR PENGUIN!*

IT ALL ADDS UP TO... *HIM!*

THE *PENGUIN*--!

YES, THE *PENGUIN*--

--NEXT TO THE *JOKER,* THE GREATEST CRIMINAL GENIUS WE'VE EVER TACKLED!

AUK! HOW *DARE* YOU TOUCH MY PRIVATE *PET*--?

HE'S A *NOBLE* CREATURE... DELICATE, SENSITIVE!

I MEANT HIM NO *HARM!*

5

6

TWO MORNINGS LATER... GOSSAMER FINGERS OF MIST CARESS THE STEEL-GRAY SEA AND THE WIND BITES PLAYFULLY AS A PAIR OF CAPED FIGURES SURVEYS AN *AWESOME* SCENE--

READY FOR A ROUGH CLIMB, ROBIN?

WITH THE YOUNG KING A *CAPTIVE,* WE DON'T *DARE* STORM THE *FRONT* OF HIS CASTLE!

SO WE ENTER VIA THE *BACK*-- UP THE SIDE OF THAT *CLIFF!*

I'M BEGINNING TO WISH I'D SPENT THIS SPRING VACATION WORKING ON MY *STAMP COLLECTION!*

YOU'RE *SURE* THE KING IS BEING HELD IN HIS OWN *PALACE?*

I'M NOT *POSITIVE*--

--BUT I'LL GIVE YOU *BIG* ODDS HE IS! REMEMBER...THE *PENGUIN LOVES* CRIME-FICTION-- HE ROOTS FOR THE *BAD GUYS!*

HE'S *PARTICULARLY* FOND OF EDGAR ALLAN POE'S *"PURLOINED LETTER,"* THE STORY ABOUT A MISSING PAPER THAT'S WHERE THE HERO LEAST *EXPECTS* IT--

--RIGHT IN *PLAIN SIGHT!* NOBODY EXPECTS THE *PENGUIN* TO HIDE THE KING AT HIS *PALACE!*

ALSO...THE CASTLE IS CALLED *"ZU DLOM"* IN THE NATIVE LANGUAGE --MEANING APPROXIMATELY, *"ROOST OF WINGS"!*

"ROOST OF WINGS"...CHECK! THE *PENGUIN WOULDN'T* BE ABLE TO RESIST *THAT!*

ROBIN...*LOOK!* EAGLE'S NEST AND THREE *ROPES* DANGLING NEARBY!

I DON'T KNOW WHAT IT *MEANS,* BUT IT GIVES ME A *CHILL!*

7

SHEW! I thought we'd NEVER reach the top--

QUIET! A couple of PLAYMATES are heading our way!

THE PENGUIN'S A NUT CASE, BUT HE PAYS GOOD--

--AND ME, I GO WHERE THE BREAD IS!

WE DO THE GOOD OLD STOMP-THE-GUARD ROUTINE?

WHAT ELSE?

ONLY PLEASE... NO BAD PUNS!

AWW... I HAVEN'T PUNNED FOR YEARS!--NOT SINCE I WAS A BOY WONDER!

US TEEN WONDERS ARE DIGNIFIED... MATURE!

I CAN'T TELL YOU HOW GLAD I AM!

HUNGRY, CHUM?

HAVE A KNUCKLE SANDWICH!

ROBIN... OWTCH!

SORRY! COULDN'T RESIST!

8

LET'S *NAIL* HIM BEFORE YOU MAKE *ANOTHER* LOUSY JOKE!

COME *ON!* THE *PENGUIN* MUST BE *INSIDE!*

MINUTES LATER, IN A LAVISH DINING HALL...

MMMM... *FISH!* *SHELLFISH!* *SQUID!* *OCTOPUS!* WE *LOVE* SEAFOOD--

DON'T WE, CHUM?

I'M *COLD!* CAN YOU NOT PROVIDE SOME *WARMTH?*

SILENCE, MOTOR MOUTH! WE *LIKE* THE COLD!

WHINE *AGAIN,* AND I'LL FEED YOU TO THE *EELS!*

AT LEAST PERMIT ME TO GIVE HIM A *BLANKET--*

--UNLIKE *YOURSELF,* HE IS *WARM-BLOODED!*

YOU'LL GIVE THE CHATTERING CHUMP EXACTLY *ZERO* UNLESS YOU HAVE MY *PERMISSION--*

--WHICH YOU *HAVEN'T!*

THE *SERVING GIRL....!* HER *MOVEMENTS--* FLUID AS *QUICKSILVER...* UNMISTAKABLY *GRACEFUL--*

9

143

--AND THE *VOICE*... LIKE SUN-WARMED *HONEY!*

IT'S HER!

I'M *TIRED* OF YOUR INFERNAL *INTERFERENCE!* I BELIEVE I'LL TEACH YOU A *LACHRYMOSE* LESSON!

--GET YOUR CLAMMY HANDS *OFF* HER--

--OR I'LL *BEND* YOU TILL YOU *BREAK!*

STAND *BACK,* *BATMAN!*

MY UMBRELLA'S FERRULE IS *RAZOR SHARP!* I'LL *SKEWER* THE FRANGIBLE FEMALE!

MY, MY! LISTEN TO THE DICTIONARY-RUN-AMOK *THREATEN!*

AUK!-- HELPERS! HENCHMEN!

10

HELP! BRING GUNS ...KNIVES...AXES--

THE OLD BUMP-THE-BADDIES ROUTINE, BATMAN?

CORRECT! AND AFTERWARD, MAYBE WE'LL PLAY PULVERIZE-THE-PENGUIN!

YOU HOLLERED, BOSS?

SOK!

SOK!

AS WE USED TO SAY... THE JIG IS UP!

NOT JUST YET, YOU MORDANT MEDDLER! I HAVE AN ALLY-- MY PRECIOUS PET!

CHUM... ATTACK! SIC 'IM!

PENGUIN, YOU'VE GOT TO BE KIDDING! OR TOTALLY FLIPPED!

YOU THINK A CUDDLY REFUGEE FROM A TUXEDO TAILOR CAN BOTHER ME?

11

However, with unexpected SPEED, the PENGUIN'S "ALLY" sinks his beak into THE BATMAN'S foot--

UNFRIENDLY BEASTIE, ISN'T HE? COME HERE...

OWTCH!

B-BATMAN... SUDDENLY FEEL DIZZY!

ME... TOO...

YOU SURELY SHOULD! MY BUDDY'S BILL IS TIPPED WITH POISON...A CURARE EXTRACT!

YOU'LL SLEEP-- BUT NOT RESTFULLY, I SHOULD ADD!

BATMAN!

PERHAPS, IN THIS LAST TORTURED MOMENT OF CONSCIOUSNESS, THE BATMAN HEARS THE TEARFUL MURMUR, FEELS THE STRONG, VELVETY ARMS...

DARLING, DARLING--

12

YOU'RE *FOND* OF HIM, EH? *EXCELLENT!* YOU'LL *JOIN* HIM AT THE *EAGLE'S NEST!*

YOU'LL ALL *THREE* SWING, SUFFER... AND *SCREAM!*

STUNG BY SALT-LADEN WIND, THE TRIO AWAKENS AND...

WE CAUGHT OURSELVES A BAD CASE OF *DANGER!* WHAT'S THE *PENGUIN'S PROGRAM,* I WONDER--

--LEAVE US TO *STARVE?*

NO! OBSERVE THE *NEST* BELOW-- THE INFANT *EAGLES!* THEIR *MOTHER* WILL RETURN...

...AND SHE'LL THINK WE'RE *THREATENING* HER LITTLE ONES! SHE'LL CLAW US TO *RIBBONS!*

YES... IT IS THE *TRADITIONAL* METHOD OF EXECUTION IN *SWAWAK!*

YOU *RECOGNIZED* ME?

I REALIZE I SHOULDN'T BE MAKING *SMALL TALK,* TALIA, BUT--

ANYWHERE, ANYTIME! I OWE YOU MY *LIFE!*

I'M CURIOUS AS TO WHY *YOU'RE* ON *KING PEEBLE'S* ISLAND!

I POSED AS A *SERVANT* TO LEARN THE STATE OF *SWAWAK'S TREASURY!*

⑬

THE *TWO* OF US WILL DIVIDE THE BIRD'S *ATTENTION*... AND DOUBLE OUR *CHANCES!*

AS THE BATTLE RAGES, THE *PENGUIN* OBSERVES FROM A RAMPART OF THE CASTLE--AND SQUAWKS IN THE FURY...

AUK! THE *CRETINOUS* *CRUSADER* AND HIS *TROUBLESOME TEEN* ARE *CHEATING!* QUICK-- GIVE ME A *RIFLE!*

I'LL *PUNCTURE* THEIR *PERFIDIOUS* PERSONS--

YEOWWWCH!

AUK! I'LL TAN YOUR *ROYAL HIDE--!*

YOU WILL NOT STEP *NEAR* ME-- NOR WILL YOU ATTEMPT TO HARM MY FRIEND THE *SERVANT!*

--OR I WILL LEAP FROM THE WALL TO THE *ROCKS* ON THE BEACH BELOW!

15

WITHOUT MY *SIGNATURE,* THE DOCUMENT YOU REQUIRE WILL BE *INVALID!*

YOUR HOPE OF BECOMING AN *EMPEROR* WILL DIE WITH ME!

AUUUU-KK!

AND ON THE LEDGE...

AT *LAST...* I'M *LOOSE!*

HOW YOU *DOING,* BATMAN?

NOT *GOOD,* KID!

CAN'T HOLD OUT MUCH... *LONGER!* WE'RE NEAR *EXHAUSTION...*

--AND *MOMMA EAGLE* IS STILL GOING *STRONG!*

I *HATE* TO DO THIS... SHE'S ONLY FOLLOWING HER *INSTINCT,* PRO-TECTING HER *YOUNG*--

--BUT IT'S *HER* OR *US!*

ZAP!

16

SLOWLY, THE SUN SINKS, AND A CHILL TOUCHES THE ISLAND, AS...

COME ON, *KIDDY KING*-- I'M A FRIENDLY FELLA WHEN YOU *UNDERSTAND* ME! I'LL GIVE YOU CANDY--

THE AMERICANS HAVE AN EXPRESSION: *"SCRAM, BUSTER!"*

AUUK! I'LL *COOK* YOUR CONTEMPTIBLE CARCASS--!

NO!

YOU'RE THE ONE WHO'S *COOKED,* PENGUIN!

AUUK! THE BLASTED *BATMAN!*

I'M IN NO MOOD TO TRADE *REPARTEE* WITH YOU!

I'LL ASK YOU-- JUST *ONCE*-- SURRENDER!

MY *FRIEND!* THANK THE HEAVENS YOU'RE *SAFE*...

YOUR *MAJESTY*... BE CAREFUL-- YOU'LL *FALL!*

EXCITED, FULL OF *DELIGHT* AT SEEING *TALIA,* KING *PEEBLE IV* TOPPLES OFF AND DOWNWARD...

OH-- OH!!

17

19

AN ALMOST LEGENDARY FIGURE, THE COWLED SHADOW OF THE BATMAN PROWLS THROUGH THE NIGHT, PREYING UPON THE CRIMINAL PARASITE LIKE THE WINGED CREATURE WHOSE NAME HE HAS ADOPTED!

CREATED BY BOB KANE

SO MUCH FOR PROF. STRANGE!

YEAH! FUNNY HOW HE WOULDN'T GIVE UP THE BATMAN'S SECRET I.D.!

GUESS HE WAS ONE OF THOSE TURKEYS WHO'S SCARED OF BATS! I DON'T UNDERSTAND GUYS LIKE THAT!

TURKEYS? NO, NO TURKEYS IN THIS ISSUE--BUT THERE'S ANOTHER SORT OF JAILBIRD WAITING IN THE WINGS. IN FACT, EVEN THOUGH WE'RE JUST DEALING WITH THUGS SO FAR, WE'VE NAMED OUR TALE--

"THE MALAY PENGUIN!"

STEVE ENGLEHART ★ STORY
MARSHALL ROGERS ★ ART

TERRY AUSTIN ★ EMBELLISHER
M. SNAPINN ★ LETTERER

JULIUS SCHWARTZ ★ EDITOR

WHERE'D HE COME FROM? WHAT IS THIS?

DON'T FREEZE, BRUNO! HE'S GOT ROBIN WITH HIM!

I NEED HELP!

BUT HE-- I JUST MENTIONED HIS NAME--!

SORRY, BRUNO! TIME'S UP!

S OK

SLAM

SPLASH

WHAT WAS THAT YOU PUSHED OFF THE PIER, MURDOCK?

KPOW KPOW

ANSWER ME!

NO! GET AWAY! AAAGH! MY HAND!

I COULDN'T *HEAR* YOU BEFORE IN THE *FOG*, SO YOU'RE GOING TO *REPEAT* IT FOR ME *NOW!*

NO, I SAID! YOU KNOW WHO I *WORK* FOR, BATMAN!

YOU CAN'T MAKE *ANYTHING* STICK!

MR. MURDOCK IS SPEAKING OF OUR *BELOVED* CITY COUNCIL PRESIDENT, RUPERT THORNE, ROBIN!

YOU'VE *MISSED* OUT ON GOTHAM'S CHANGING *POLITICAL* FORTUNES!

BUT I'VE READ THE *PAPERS*--BETWEEN THE *LINES!* DOES THORNE *REALLY* CONTROL THE *POLICE?*

NO--NOT WITH *COMMISSIONER GORDON* IN CHARGE! HE CONTROLS THE *COURTS!*

AND THE POLICE IN MATTERS OF CITY POLICY--

EEEE EEEEE EEEEE

--LIKE WHETHER *THE BATMAN'S* STILL *WELCOME* IN GOTHAM CITY!

HERE *COME* THE POLICE--AND I'M READY TO MEET THEM WITH *OPEN ARMS!* HOW ABOUT *YOU,* BATMAN?

EEEEE

PIER-31 WAREHOUSE

LET'S GET *OUT* OF HERE!

③

--TO THE PENGUIN!

THE AUCTION WAS TO BE *TONIGHT*-- BUT I AM *ALONE!* NOT EVEN MY *COMPETITORS* HAVE APPEARED!

IS THIS A *GAME?* AND IF *SO*-- WHAT ARE THE *RULES?*

WELL, I HAVE *LITTLE TIME* TO DEVOTE TO THE MATTER *NOW*, WITH MY *PRIMARY PLANS* PROCEEDING *APACE!*

LEARNING *THE BATMAN'S* SECRET WOULD HAVE BEEN *GLORIOUS*, BUT IT SEEMS NOT TO *BE!*

IF ONLY I KNEW WHO MY *RIVALS* WERE--!

HA HA HA HA HA HA

IT RAINS DOWN LIKE ICE CUBES, THAT LAUGH--

--THE MAD LAUGH OF--

THE JOKER!

SHOW YOURSELF--

--YOU GRINNING GARGOYLE!

THE PENGUIN FEARS NO *SANE* MAN-- BUT *THE JOKER* IS HARDLY *THAT!*

IT'S HIGH TIME I TOOK MY *LEAVE!*

AT LEAST, I KNOW *HE* DIDN'T DIVERT *STRANGE!* HE WOULDN'T RETURN *HERE* IF HE *HAD!*

WE HAVE *NO NEED* TO *CROSS SWORDS*--

--AND THAT SUITS ME *PERFECTLY!*

SHAKE A LEG, BOYS! WE HAVE PLACES TO GO!

Gotham News

READ THE NEWS WEEKLY

THUMP

Gotham News

SUPERMAN CAPTUR

REED GALLERIES TO EXHIBIT LEGENDARY MALAY PENGUIN

BY MAUREEN LIBE

GOTHAM--(AP)-The R Malay Penguin next

AND, IN THE REED GALLERIES...

HOW COULD YOU *DO* SOMETHING LIKE THIS, REED?

REED

MY DEAR *BATMAN!* WHAT ARE YOU TALKING ABOUT?

THIS *JEWELED BIRD* YOUR GALLERY'S PUTTING ON DISPLAY-- *THAT'S* WHAT! DON'T YOU KNOW THE *REAL* PENGUIN *BROKE JAIL* THREE WEEKS AGO? *

AM I TO UNDERSTAND THAT THE *WORLD OF ART* IS TO BE RULED BY THAT *ODD LITTLE MAN* WITH THE *PECULIAR ROLLING GAIT?*

THE *REED GALLERIES* IS AN *EXHIBITION HALL!* WE *EXHIBIT* THINGS! THERE IS NOTHING MORE TO *SAY!*

* AFTER HIS CAPTURE IN *BATMAN #288!*--JULIE

6

WHAT CONCERN IS IT OF *YOURS*, ANYWAY? YOU NO LONGER HAVE ANY OFFICIAL STATUS IN THIS CITY!

LISTEN, MR. REED--!

NO, *YOU* LISTEN! I CAN'T SAY I *APPROVE* OF THE CITY'S RESOLUTION, BUT I WILL *NOT BE DICTATED* TO IN MY *OWN* GALLERY! I ASSURE YOU, OUR SECURITY IS *QUITE SUFFICIENT!*

SEE HERE--

--THE MALAY PENGUIN REPOSES IN ITS *OWN ROOM*--

--TO BE VIEWED ONLY AT A *DISTANCE* THROUGH *MAGNIFYING WINDOWS!*

SURROUNDING THE *BIRD ITSELF*--

CLICK

--IS A RING OF *LASERS* AND *ELECTRONIC EYES!*

THAT CAN BE *BEATEN!* THE *SHADOW-THIEF* DID SO *--!

*IN JLA #139 --JULIE

CLICK!

AH! BUT *FIRST*, THE PENGUIN WOULD HAVE TO WALK ACROSS THE *FLOOR*-- WHICH IS MONITORED BY *SEISMO*-- *GRAPHS* TO DETECT *VIBRATION!*

HE COULDN'T *FLY* BECAUSE THERE ARE *MICROPHONES* TO PICK OUT ANY *UNTOWARD NOISE*-- EVEN THE *WHIRR* OF WINGS!

WHAT ABOUT *TELEVISION CAMERAS?*

CAM-RAS?

BATMAN, LET'S BE *REALISTIC* HERE! THERE *IS* SUCH A THING AS *OVERKILL*-- AND THERE *IS* SUCH A THING AS A *BUDGET!*

WHO DO YOU THINK THE *PENGUIN* IS ANYWAY-- A *GHOST?*

I THINK THE *PENGUIN* IS A MAN WHO LOVES TO *PLAY GAMES*--CHALLENGING GAMES! HE LOVES TO MATCH WITS FOR *HIGH STAKES*--PARTICULARLY *PRICELESS BIRDS!*

I *THINK*, MR. REED, THAT THE *PENGUIN* IS NOT A MAN TO BE *UNDER-ESTIMATED*--BUDGET OR NO BUDGET!

⑦

LATER, IN BRUCE WAYNE'S PENTHOUSE...

DICK, I HATE PEOPLE WHO KNOW THEY KNOW IT ALL! WE'VE GOT HUGO STRANGE ON ONE HAND, AND NOW, BECAUSE OF REED, WE'VE GOT THE PENGUIN ON THE OTHER!

AND WE'RE SUPPOSED TO HAVE OUR HANDS TIED!

SIR, THE MORNING REPORT FROM YOUR ATTORNEYS HAS ARRIVED!

SUMMARIZE IT, PLEASE, ALFRED!

WELL, SIR, SINCE HUGO STRANGE LEFT ALL THE MONEY HE DRAINED FROM YOUR HOLDINGS HERE AT THE OFFICE WHEN HE DISAPPEARED, THEY FEEL MOST OF HIS DEALINGS CAN BE NULLIFIED!

WALL STREET WILL BREATHE MORE EASILY WITH WAYNE ENTERPRISES BACK IN ITS ACCUSTOMED POSITION!

THAT'S GOOD! WHAT ABOUT THE MAIL?

NOTHING IMPORTANT.

THANK-YOU'S, REQUESTS-- ANNOUNCEMENT OF A BOARD MEETING IN PARIS BY YOUR SECURITY EXCHANGE--

PARIS, HUH? THAT WOULD SOUND GOOD ANY TIME BUT NOW!

I'LL SEND BROOME! HE'S A GOOD MAN!

GOOD NIGHT, ALFRED!

GOOD MORNING, SIR!

I'LL AWAKEN YOU AT NOON!

NOON COMES ALL TOO SOON, BUT BRUCE CANNOT SLEEP IN! EVEN TO A FINANCIAL VETERAN, THE RESTORATION OF AN EMPIRE IS NO MEAN FEAT!

WE'LL BE GOING OUT ON PATROL, DICK--BUT FIRST, I HAVE A STOP TO MAKE!

BUT HE TACKLES IT IN HIS STRIDE-- AND WHEN FIVE O'CLOCK COMES, HE'S JUST FINDING HIS SECOND WIND...

K 2263

B

GOTHAM GENERAL--?

YES, SILVER'S IN HERE!* THEY'VE STARTED TO ALLOW HER VISITORS!

HAM GENERAL HOSPITA

* SILVER ST. CLOUD, BRUCE'S CURRENT FLAME, WAS ALSO CAPTURED BY HUGO STRANGE LAST TIME! --JULIE

HELLO, SILVER--

HI, BRUCE! WOW! YOU'RE LOOKING GOOD!

THEY'VE KEPT ME HERE FOR TWO DAYS SO FAR-- AFRAID I GOT SOME OF THAT MONSTER SERUM ALL THOSE OTHER POOR PEOPLE GOT! I THOUGHT YOU'D BE IN BED, TOO!

NO SUCH LUCK!

I'M A WORKING MAN!

HI! YOU MUST BE BRUCE'S WARD, DICK!

UM...YEAH! I WANT TO APOLOGIZE FOR BRUSHING YOU OFF THE OTHER NIGHT--!*

NEVER MIND!

I SUPPOSE I DID SOUND PRETTY LOONY!

* DICK ONLY PRETENDED TO DO THAT LAST ISSUE, SO HE COULD CHANGE TO ROBIN! --JULIE

BUT YOU WERE RIGHT, SILVER! YOU SAVED MY LIFE, AND THAT'S WHAT COUNTS!

I THINK THAT'S MY EXIT CUE! I'LL BE WAITING OUTSIDE!

OOO-WHEE!

9

164

THAT TAKES CARE OF BRUCE'S DAYLIGHT HOURS!
LATER, WHEN NIGHT MANTLES THE CITY, HE GREETS HIS OTHER LOVE...
GOTHAM
...ADVENTURE!
THE GALLERIES LOOK PRETTY QUIET, BATMAN!
WE'LL JUST WATCH FOR A WHILE!
ROBIN! COMING OUT OF THE THEATER...!
GOT YOU, BATMAN! I'D RECOGNIZE THAT WADDLING WALK ANYWHERE--
--THE PENGUIN!
EGAD! B and R!
DON'T YOU EVER GET TIRED OF BREAKING JAIL, PENGUIN?
NOT AS TIRED AS I GET BEING PUT THERE, BATMAN!
LET ME EXHIBIT HOW I DID IT--WITH MY BUZZ-UMBRELLA!
WITHOUT WORD OR LOOK, THE DYNAMIC DUO RESPONDS AS ONE!
PFAH! MISSED!
10

--BUT I DIDN'T!

THEN PERMIT ME TO DEMONSTRATE WHAT YOU *HAVE* MISSED, ROBIN! THE SPEED-CONTROL ON MY BLADES!

I HAVE BUT TO *USE* IT...

...TO *LOSE* YOUR *ANNOYING* ATTENTIONS!

PERHAPS *NOT*, PENGUIN!

SORRY, BATMAN! THIS BIRD HAS *FLOWN!*

BUT UNTIL WE MEET AGAIN, REMEMBER--

--NEVER PITCH *ROLLS* AT A *BANK!*

HUH?!

NOW, LET US TURN FOR A MOMENT TO MATTERS AT THE FAMED *TOBACCONISTS' CLUB...* MATTERS WHICH WILL ALSO AFFECT THIS SAGA MOST PROFOUNDLY...

NO! I NEVER AGREED TO *MURDER!*

YOU AGREED TO MY *PLAN*, DR. BELL!

YES--TO RID US OF *THE BATMAN*, YOU SAID! BUT YOU NEVER MENTIONED *MURDER!*

I *TOLD* YOU THE DOC HAD *SCRUPLES*, RUPE!

HUGO STRANGE MAY HAVE BEEN A *CRIMINAL--!*

YEAH! AND A *WEAK LIVER!*

11

WH-WHAT--?

YOU HAVEN'T BEEN ON THE COUNCIL FOR VERY LONG, DOCTOR! I SUPPOSE I SHOULD HAVE STARTED WORRYING...

...WHEN PHOSPHORUS SPOOKED YOU SO EASY! *

*DETECTIVE #469! -- JULIE

THIS COUNCIL HAS TO WORK CLOSELY TOGETHER, DOCTOR-- VERY CLOSELY!

TAKE HIM AWAY, MURDOCK!

BUT THEN, SUDDENLY...

GO ON--TAKE HIM, THORNE! TAKE HIM AS YOU TOOK ME!

BUT SOON-- I SHALL TAKE YOU!

WHA--? WHAT--?!?

SOMETHING THE MATTER, RUPE?

YOU--YOU DIDN'T SEE--

--ANYTHING?

SEE ANYTHING? WHATTA YOU MEAN?

I THOUGHT-- I MEAN--

--FORGET IT! WHAT ARE YOU ALL GAWKING AT?

12

166

MEANWHILE, BACK AT *THE BATMAN*--

A BATTLE OF *WITS*--

--FOUGHT WITH *UMBRELLAS, BIRDS,* AND *WORDS!* IT'S ALWAYS THE SAME-- AND ALWAYS *DIFFERENT!*

"NEVER PITCH *ROLLS* AT A *BANK!*"

AN ALARM--FROM THE *REED GALLERIES!*

HOW'D THAT BIRD *DO* IT? WE JUST CHASED HIM *AWAY!*

HOWEVER, WHEN BATMAN AND ROBIN BURST INTO THE HALL...

WELL, I ADMIRE YOUR *PROMPTNESS*, GENTLEMEN-- BUT YOU'VE ANSWERED A *FALSE ALARM!*

TUNK TA-TA-TUNK

YOU HEAR *THAT?*

THE *THEATER* NEXT DOOR IS REHEARSING A *NEW MUSICAL*--

--WITH A *HERD* OF *ELEPHANTS*, IT SOUNDS LIKE! THE *VIBRATION* AND *SOUND* SET OFF THE *SEISMOGRAPHS* AND THE *MICROPHONES!*

I THINK I'LL *SUE!*

HOW ARE WE GOING TO KEEP OUR *TRAPS* SET IF--

WHY, THEY'RE *GONE!*

TUNKATA TUNKATA

ONLY NEXT DOOR, MR. REED...

TUNK TA-TA-TUNK TUNKA TUNK

JNK TUNKA TA-TA-TUNK!

TA-TUNK TUNKA TUNKA

A-TUNK T

LET'S SEE THESE "ELEPHANTS"--

WOW! DUMBO WAS *NEVER* LIKE THIS!

13

167

TAKE *FIVE*, GIRLS! LOOK WHO'S COME TO *VISIT* US!

BATMAN AND ROBIN! I DON'T SUPPOSE YOU'D CARE TO *ENDORSE* OUR LITTLE *EXTRAVAGANZA*?

THORNE'S CAMPAIGN DOESN'T SEEM TO HAVE HAD MUCH EFFECT ON THE *PEOPLE*, AT LEAST!

I HAVE ONLY ONE QUESTION, SIR: WHO'S *BACKING* THE SHOW?

FUNNY YOU SHOULD ASK, BATMAN--

--BECAUSE I DON'T *KNOW*!

WE GET OUR MONEY THROUGH THE *FIRST GOTHAM BANK*!

I FIGURE HE'S ONE OF THOSE *PUBLICITY-SHY* BILLIONAIRES--

--YOU *KNOW*--

--A REAL *MYSTERY MAN*!

THANKS *VERY MUCH*! YOU'VE BEEN A GREAT HELP!

I HAVE--?

THINK YOU'VE GOT THE ANSWER, FRIENDS? THEN PLAY ALONG WITH US A FEW MOMENTS LONGER, AS WE SHIFT TO THE FOLLOWING EVENING...

...ATOP WAYNE FOUNDATION--

"NEVER PITCH ROLLS AT A BANK"?

GOOD LUCK IN *PARIS*, BROOME!

GOOD LUCK ON THE *PLANE*, YOU MEAN, MR. *WAYNE*! MOST ALL OF THE *AMERICAN EXCHANGE* MEMBERS WILL BE *FLYING* OVER WITH ME, AND I'LL BE *NEGOTIATING* ALL THE WAY!

YOU CAN HANDLE THEM, BROOME, I'M SURE!

SO LONG!

WHAT IN THE *WORLD*--?

GEESE--FLYING IN THE FORM OF THE *PENGUIN'S* PROFILE!

THEY'RE *DROPPING* SOMETHING-- ALL ACROSS THE *CITY*!

14

LOOK OUT!

LEAFLETS!

CLANG

CLATTER

--ATTACHED TO SOMETHING!

GOLD COINS! DOUBLE EAGLES--$20 GOLD PIECES! THE GOVERNMENT HASN'T MINTED THESE SINCE THE 30'S!

THE PENGUIN SURE WANTED THIS AIR-DROP NOTICED!

OF COURSE--SINCE THESE NOTES ARE ALL IDENTICAL LETTERS TO THE BATMAN!

BATMAN, WE NEED STALL NO LONGER! TIME IS ON THE WING! TONIGHT I SHALL LIFT THE SILVER BIRD--AND YOU WILL TAKE A DIVE!

DISRESPECTFULLY YOURS--

The Penguin

THEN WE'VE GOT HIM! IT ALL FITS!

HE BACKS THE MUSICAL, TO MESS UP THE GALLERIES' ALARMS SO THAT HE CAN MAKE A RAID IN THE CONFUSION!

SNAP!

I DON'T KNOW WHAT THAT "PITCH ROLLS" BUSINESS MEANS, BUT THE MONEY COMES THROUGH A "BANK," AND THE DANCERS--THE "CHICKS"--ARE FEATHERED LIKE BIRDS!

JUST LIKE YOU ALWAYS SAID, THE PENGUIN'S WEAK SPOT IS HIS VANITY! HE THINKS HE CAN PLAY WITH US--BUT WE'VE OUTSMARTED HIM!

RIGHT--?

WRONG!

15

GOTHAM INTERNATIONAL AIRPORT--

SKREEE --

THE BATMAN!

GET AWAY FROM THE PLANE! WE'RE ABOUT TO TAKE OFF!

SKREEEEEEF

BUT THE DARK KNIGHT MAKES NO REPLY!

HE SPRINTS UP THE STAIRWAY--

--DUCKS PAST THE STEWS--

--AND POUNDS PURPOSEFULLY THROUGH THE CLUSTERED CABIN--

--UNTIL HE REACHES THE COCKPIT!

GOOD LORD! THE WORD'S OUT ON THE BATMAN!

HE'S HIJACKING THE PLANE!

WRONG!

HE IS!

¡AWRRK!

THE PENGUIN!

YOU WERE RIGHT--

--BUT--

--I DON'T GET IT!

I WAS SO SURE HE WAS AFTER THE MALAY STATUE!

16

170

THAT'S WHAT WE WERE *SUPPOSED* TO THINK, *ROBIN!* HE SPARED *NO EXPENSE* TO FOCUS OUR *ATTENTION* ON THAT BIRD--

--BACKING THE *MUSICAL,* AS YOU *SURMISED*--

--LURKING AROUND THE *THEATER* UNTIL WE *SPOTTED* HIM-- ALL OF THAT!

HE HAD *ME* FOOLED, TOO -- FOR A WHILE!

BUT THOUGH *THE PENGUIN PLAYS GAMES,* HE ALWAYS PLAYS *FAIR!* THINK OF THE *WORDS* HE USED WHENEVER HE SENT US A *MESSAGE*-- OUT OF THEIR *CONTEXT!*

"*PITCH,*" "*ROLL,*" "*BANK*"--AND THEN "*STALL,*" "*WING,*" "*LIFT,*" AND "*DIVE*"!

OF COURSE...!

THEY'RE ALL *FLIGHT* WORDS!

AND THERE WAS *NOTHING* ABOUT THE *MALAY STATUE* INVOLVING *FLIGHT*-- NOT EVEN THE *BIRD* ITSELF, BECAUSE PENGUINS *CAN'T FLY*--

--UNLESS THEY STEAL A "*SILVER BIRD*" CALLED AN *AIRPLANE!*

AS SOON AS THE *SECOND MESSAGE* CAME, I REALIZED WE'D BEEN *DECOYED*-- AND THE ONLY *AIRPLANE* I KNEW THAT WAS *WORTH HIJACKING* WAS *THIS* ONE -- FILLED WITH MEMBERS OF THE *SECURITIES EXCHANGE,* ON THEIR WAY TO *PARIS!*

INCREDIBLE! WHAT A *PLAN!*

AND YET-- IT SEEMS *HARD* TO IMAGINE THE PENGUIN PASSING UP THE *MALAY BIRD!*

WHO SAID ANYTHING ABOUT *PASSING IT UP,* TWERP?

I STOLE IT *TWO WEEKS AGO,* BEFORE IT EVEN *GOT* TO THIS COUNTRY!

THE ONE IN THE *GALLERY* IS A *FAKE!*

COME ON, PENGUIN! YOU'RE GOING BACK TO YOUR *CAGE!*

INCREDIBLE! I'M OUT ON MY OWN...

...MAKING MY OWN WAY IN THE WORLD, AND NOT DOING A *BAD JOB* OF IT, EITHER...

...BUT WHEN IT COMES TO *THE BATMAN,* I'VE GOT A *LONG WAY* TO GO!

Fin

GOTHAM CITY FIRST METHODIST CHURCH, JULY 6, 8:45 P.M....

...AND DO YOU, SELINA KYLE, TAKE THIS MAN, BRUCE WAYNE, TO BE YOUR LAWFULLY WEDDED HUSBAND?

I DO.... OH, YES, I DO!

I NOW PRONOUNCE YOU MAN AND WIFE...YOU MAY KISS THE BRIDE.

DARLING...

BRUCE DEAREST... ≈choke≈ I-I'VE NEVER BEEN AS HAPPY AS I AM AT THIS MOMENT!

BRAVO! AT LAST!

CONGRATULATIONS, YOU TWO!

THOUGHT IT WOULD NEVER HAPPEN!

HOORAY!

YOU'RE A LUCKY MAN, BRUCE!

DON'T I KNOW IT!

AND I'M GOING TO EXERCISE AN ANCIENT PRIVILEGE...

...AND KISS THE NEW BRIDE!

THAT IS IF BRUCE DOESN'T MI-- GOOD LORD!

SELINA, NO!

WHA--WHAT IS IT? WHAT'S WRONG?

W-WHY ARE YOU ALL STARING AT ME?

MY GOD! LOOK AT HER!

IT'S TRUE! IT'S TRUE! SHE IS A CAT!

DARLING, YOU PROMISED!

SHE'LL ALWAYS BE A CAT!

DISGUSTING! KILL HER!

YES, KILL THE WRETCHED CREATURE!

NO! PLEASE!

MY GOD!

1

173

TERROR TRAIN!

NNOOOOOOOEEEEEEEEEE!

POW! POW! BLAM!

NO!! =Gasp!=

GOTHAM CITY AMTRAK, FIFTY MILES DUE WEST, JULY 6, 8:45 P.M....

BRUCE JONES, STORY
TREVOR VON EEDEN
& PABLO MARCOS, ART
TODD KLEIN, LETTERS
HELEN VESIK COLORS
DICK GIORDANO, EDITOR

MISS? ER...ARE YOU ALL RIGHT?

WHA? OH...YES, I ...EXCUSE ME. I-I HAD A DREAM...A NIGHTMARE ...I'M QUITE ALL RIGHT, THANK YOU...

=whew= HOW HIDEOUS! I'M SURE FREUD WOULD HAVE A FIELD DAY WITH THAT LITTLE DOOZY!

I NEED A DRINK! CLUB CAR'S THIS WAY, I THINK...

=SIGH= BRUCE...I CAN'T GET MY MIND OFF YOU, EVEN IN MY SLEEP...

PARDON ME...

2

AH, CATWOMAN, AT LAST! GLAD YOU COULD MAKE IT!

PLEASE...ER... HAVE A SEAT...

THE NAME'S ≈UMPHH≈ SELINA KYLE...

YES, OF COURSE, FORGIVE ME, AND FORGIVE THE WAY I HAD YOU BROUGHT HERE. WE WEREN'T CERTAIN YOU'D...AH...COOPERATE.

THUD

I'M DETECTIVE SERGEANT RICHARD STUART, MISS KYLE, I--

I'M CLEAN, SERGEANT.

EH? YES, OF COURSE. WE KNOW THAT. THIS ISN'T AN ARREST, MISS KYLE... IT'S MORE LIKE A... PROPOSAL.

HENRY?

HAVE A LOOK AT THIS, MISS KYLE...

THE VANISHING TRAINS CASE... YES, I'VE HEARD OF IT.

THERE'S BEEN A THIRD DISAPPEARANCE?

NOT YET. BUT AMTRAK 419 IS SCHEDULED TO RUN TOMORROW AT TWELVE NOON: DESTINATION, CHICAGO. WE WANT TO BE SURE IT DOESN'T SHARE THE SAME FATE AS 417 AND 418.

2ND PASSENGER TRAIN VANISHES! POLICE AND FBI BAFFLED!

AND YOU WANT MY HELP?

WE WANT THE BEST, CATWO--UH, MISS KYLE. YOU'RE THE BEST.

I'M FLATTERED.

SO WHAT WOULD YOU HAVE ME DO?

HERE'S A MAP OF THE AREA THE TRAINS COVER--OR ARE *SUPPOSED* TO COVER. AS YOU KNOW, THE LAST TWO VANISHED COMPLETELY SOMEWHERE BETWEEN GOTHAM AND CHICAGO, ILLINOIS...ONLY TO TURN UP FIVE DAYS LATER, INTACT, ALL PASSENGERS ACCOUNTED FOR...

WHAT DID THE PASSENGERS SAY?

VARYING REPORTS: SOME CLAIMED TO HAVE SEEN 'GHOSTS' OR 'DEMONS', MOST COMPLAINED OF MEMORY LOSS...

...BUT *ALL* AGREED THAT AT SOME POINT ALL THE LIGHTS WENT OUT, FOLLOWED BY A LENGTHY PERIOD OF BLACKNESS.

HMM. ANY TUNNELS ALONG THE WAY WHERE A TRAIN MIGHT BE SIDETRACKED?

ONLY ONE, BUT IT'S NOT LONG ENOUGH TO HIDE A THIRTY-SIX CAR TRAIN IN.

WE'VE CHECKED OVER EVERY INCH OF THAT TRACK, HAD GUARDS POSTED EVERY OTHER MILE. FRANKLY, WE'RE STUMPED!

PETE, THAT FILM READY?

④

HERE'S SOME HELICOPTER FOOTAGE OUR BOYS TOOK DURING THE 418'S LAST RUN.

"THERE'S THAT TUNNEL I MENTIONED. AS YOU CAN SEE, THE ENGINE IS WELL OUT OF THE OTHER SIDE BEFORE THE CABOOSE IS EVEN NEAR THE ENTRANCE..."

"NOW WATCH THIS AND GET READY FOR A JOLT!"

"I-IT'S FADING...FADING INTO THIN AIR!"

"UM-M-M...AND IT'S *NOT* TRICK PHOTOGRAPHY!"

IT'S GONE! VANISHED!

JUST LIKE A GHOST!

SO YOU SEE WHAT WE'RE UP AGAINST, MISS KYLE. HALF MY STAFF REALLY BELIEVES IT IS A SUPERNATURAL OCCURRENCE!

YET THE TRAIN ALWAYS REAPPEARS SEVERAL DAYS LATER AT THE CHICAGO STATION, PASSENGERS *AND* THEIR MONEY INTACT...

EXACTLY. DOESN'T *SOUND* LIKE FOUL PLAY, DOES IT?

OR MAYBE THAT'S WHAT THEY *WANT* YOU TO THINK--WHOEVER 'THEY' ARE...

LET'S ASSUME FOR A MOMENT THAT IT *IS* A CRIMINAL PLOT OF SOME KIND... WHY WOULD THEY WANT TO MAKE A TRAIN 'DISAPPEAR' FOR A FEW DAYS WITHOUT STEALING ANYTHING FROM IT?

≈SIGH≈ I DUNNO... MAYBE WHAT WE'VE GOT HERE *IS* SOME KIND OF BERMUDA TRIANGLE THING...

SNAP!

DRUGS! THEY'RE TRANSPORTING DRUGS INTO CHICAGO!

BOTH THE 417 AND THE 418 WERE THOROUGHLY CHECKED IN THE CHICAGO STATION--THEY'RE CLEAN.

WE THOUGHT OF THAT.

5.

OKAY, SERGEANT, I'LL TAKE YOUR CASE! I'LL GET MY COSTUME OUT OF MOTHBALLS!

GREAT! HOW CAN WE HELP YOU?

GET ME RECORDS OF ALL THREE TRAINS DATING BACK TO THE DAY THEY WERE BUILT. AND AFTER THAT--

--GET ME A TICKET ON BOARD THE 419!

TIME: 2:25 P.M.

PLACE: AMTRAK RAILROAD CAR FIFTY MILES OUTSIDE OF GOTHAM.

TRAIN: THE 419.

SO FAR, SO QUIET...

ACCORDING TO THESE BLUEPRINTS AND DATA THAT DETECTIVE STUART GAVE ME, SOME OF THESE CARS WERE BUILT DURING THE SECOND WORLD WAR AND WERE REFURBISHED FOR PRESENT DAY USE BY AMTRAK.

HERE COMES THAT TUNNEL STUART SHOWED ME IN THE MOVIE...

THE LAST TRAIN DISAPPEARED SHORTLY AFTER EMERGING FROM THE OTHER SIDE.

WOW! BLACK AS PITCH IN HERE! CAN'T SEE MY HAND BEFORE MY--

HEY! SHOULDN'T I BE SEEING THE TUNNEL EXIT BY NOW?

SOMETHING SCREWY GOING ON HERE...

6

In the Land of the DEAD

THE CATWOMAN

UH...BLACKED OUT... HEAD SPLITTING... W-WHAT HAPPENED? L-LAST THING I RE- MEMBER, I WAS BEING *HANGED* BY A GHOST!

STORY:
   BRUCE JONES
ART:
   TREVOR VON EEDEN
   & PABLO MARCOS
LETTERING:
   SHELLY LEFERMAN
COLORIST:
   HELEN VESIK
EDITOR:
   DICK GIORDANO

AGHH!

NICE WEAPON, THIS CAT-O'-NINE-TAILS OF YOURS--

--I'LL SEE IF I CAN'T MAKE IT STANDARD ISSUE ON THE FORCE!

SERGEANT STUART! SO *YOU'RE* THE BRAINS BEHIND ALL THIS! IT FIGURES!

PERHAPS YOU'D CARE TO PROVIDE ME WITH SOME DETAILS...

MY PLEASURE. YOUR TRAIN, THE 419, ALREADY WENT AHEAD TO CHICAGO WITHOUT YOU! AND TWENTY EYEWITNESSES SWEAR THEY SAW YOU HANGED!

YOU SEE, YOU REALLY *ARE* DEAD!

CUTE, STUART, CUTE. BUT GET TO THE BOTTOM LINE. WHY?

"IN 1945, DURING WORLD WAR II, THERE EXISTED A CLEVER, CUNNING, BRILLIANT MAN WHO WAS ALSO A SPY FOR THE GERMAN GOVERNMENT.

HE WAS KNOWN AS THE "JEWELER" BECAUSE HE STOLE SECRET FORMULAS FROM THE AMERICANS AND TRANSCRIBED THEM, IN CODE, ONTO THE FACES OF DIAMONDS SO THAT THEY COULD NEVER BE DESTROYED... THAT MAN WAS MY FATHER.

"TOWARD THE END OF THE WAR, HE CAME BY A FORMULA THAT WOULD ASSURE GERMANY'S VICTORY, THE FORMULA FOR MAKING A HYDROGEN BOMB! HE INSCRIBED IT ONTO THE FACE OF A CAT'S-EYE DIAMOND...BUT BEFORE HE COULD LEAVE THE COUNTRY, HE REALIZED THAT HE WAS BEING FOLLOWED...

"HE DUCKED INTO A SMALL PET SHOP AND SURREPTITIOUSLY TAPED THE DIAMOND TO THE INSIDE OF THE COLLAR OF A BEAUTIFUL PERSIAN CAT...

"JUST OUTSIDE THE PET SHOP, HE WAS PICKED UP BY THE FBI...

...BUT SINCE HE WAS CLEAN, TWENTY-FOUR HOURS LATER HE WAS RELEASED..."

3

"HE RETURNED IMMEDIATELY TO THE PET STORE. THERE HE FOUND A SIGN POSTED ON THE DOOR--"

GONE TO CHICAGO FOR CAT SHOW

"...THE PERSIAN CAT WAS GONE!"

"AS HE LEFT THE SHOP, HE SAW THE PROPRIETOR HEADING TOWARD THE TRAIN STATION, AN ANIMAL CAGE BENEATH HIS ARM! ..."

"MY FATHER FOLLOWED HIM TO THE STATION, BOARDED, WAITED UNTIL THE MAN WAS NAPPING, THEN STOLE THE CAT. THE MAN AWOKE AND GAVE CHASE. MY FATHER ATTEMPTED TO ESCAPE BETWEEN THE MOVING CARS..."

SILV

"A SHORT FIGHT ENSUED ATOP ONE OF THE CARS, DURING WHICH MY FATHER WAS KNOCKED OVER THE EDGE TO HIS DEATH!"

"THE MAN WHO KILLED HIM, SELINA KYLE, WAS YOUR FATHER!"

NOTHING WAS FOUND ON MY FATHER'S BODY, NO ID, NO MONEY, NO DIAMOND! THE NEXT WEEK GERMANY FELL TO THE ALLIES. MY FATHER HAD DIED IN DISGRACE IN THE EYES OF HIS COUNTRYMEN! I EMIGRATED TO AMERICA AS A BOY. MY WHOLE LIFE HAS BEEN DEDICATED TO AVENGING MY FATHER!

I BEGAN AN ATTEMPT TO RECOVER THE DIAMOND, KNOWING MY FATHER'S PROPENSITY FOR HIDING THE INSCRIBED JEWEL DURING DANGER AND COMING BACK LATER TO RECOVER IT.

FIRST I TOOK A JOB ON THE RAILROAD, THINKING I COULD SEARCH THE TRAIN HE'D TRAVELED ON ...

I WOULD THEN CHECK EACH CAR THOROUGHLY AND SEND IT ON ITS WAY, PASSENGERS UNHARMED, NOTHING SEEMINGLY STOLEN!

BUT THEN I DISCOVERED THAT THAT TRAIN HAD BEEN DISASSEMBLED AND THE CARS FROM IT USED ON THE FOUR SEPARATE AMTRAK TRAINS THAT RUN THE CHICAGO ROUTE TODAY. SO I JOINED THE GOTHAM POLICE FORCE. MY PLANS WERE SIMPLY TO "KIDNAP" EACH TRAIN, ONE AT A TIME...

NATURALLY, AS DETECTIVE SERGEANT STUART, I MADE SURE I WAS ASSIGNED TO THE CASE OF THE "VANISHING TRAINS"...

I'M STILL WAITING...

HM...?

4

183

AH YES! *HOW* DID I MAKE THE TRAINS "VANISH" INTO THIN AIR?

IT ISN'T HARD, REALLY, WHEN YOU KNOW HOW!

SO QUIT GLOATING AND TELL ME!

① "THE SECRET IS IN THAT SMALL TUNNEL I SHOWED YOU IN THE FILM.

REAL TRAIN → →

TUNNEL

③ "THE TRAIN SEEN *EXITING* THE TUNNEL IS A HOLOGRAPHIC PROJECTION TURNED TO THE SAME SPEED AS THE REAL TRAIN. A REAL TRAIN ENTERS, A "GHOST" TRAIN EXITS!

HOLOGRAPH TRAIN

② "FOR AS THE REAL TRAIN ENTERS THE TUNNEL MOUTH, IT'S IMMEDIATELY SIDE-TRACKED INTO AN UNDERGROUND PASSAGE..."

REAL TRAIN

WHEN THE HOLOGRAPH IS TURNED OFF, THE TRAIN APPEARS TO VANISH!

I SEE. CLEVER. AND THE "GHOSTS" ON BOARD ARE HOLOGRAPHS TOO?

UH-HUH... AND HOW EXACTLY *WAS* I STRANGLED?

NERVE GAS, THE SAME AS THE OTHER PASSENGERS. SORRY ABOUT THE HEADACHE AND SLIGHT MEMORY LOSS, BUT WE DO HAVE TO COVER OUR LITTLE TRACKS.

EXACTLY, AS ARE THE TOMBSTONES OUTSIDE THE TRAIN WINDOW. OH, AND ALSO THE "NOOSE" THAT "HANGED" YOU!

AND NOW I'LL BID YOU ADIEU, SELINA KYLE...

WAIT A MINUTE! WHERE DO *I* FIT IN?

YOUR DEATH WILL AVENGE MY FATHER'S HONOR. AS DETECTIVE STUART I WAS ABLE TO CONVINCE THE COMMISSIONER THAT I SHOULD RIDE THIS LAST TRAIN, THE 420, ALONE. I WILL NOW SEARCH THE REMAINING CARS, FIND THE DIAMOND, AND RETURN THE TRAIN TO CHICAGO, PRETENDING THAT, LIKE THE OTHER PASSENGERS, I SAW ONLY GHOSTS...

AFTER THAT, I'LL TAKE THE DIAMOND WITH ITS FORMULA TO GERMANY, WHERE MY FATHER'S NAME WILL BE VINDICATED AND GERMANY WILL *RISE ONCE AGAIN WITH THE FOURTH REICH!*

I'VE *FINALLY* FIGURED OUT JUST WHAT IT IS I LIKE ABOUT YOU, BRUCE.

YOU MAKE ME *LAUGH.*

THIS MORNING AT BREAKFAST, I FELT AS IF MY WHOLE *WORLD* WERE COLLAPSING*--

*SEE LAST MONTH'S *DETECTIVE* FOR DETAILS. --Len.

--BUT AFTER A DAY WITH YOU LARKING AROUND *NEW ENGLAND*, I FEEL *SIXTEEN* AGAIN.

WHAT'S YOUR *SECRET*, MR. WAYNE?

I'M *RICH.* RICH PEOPLE DON'T TAKE *ANYTHING* SERIOUSLY.

HA.

AFTER TODAY, SELINA KYLE SEEMS LIKE A *BAD DREAM.*

I STILL FEEL *SORRY* FOR HER, OF COURSE, BUT AS YOU SAID THIS MORNING--

-- SHE HAS TO TAKE RESPONSIBILITY FOR HER *OWN* LIFE.

THAT'S WHAT I SAID...BUT IS THAT *REALLY* WHAT I FEEL? I LOVED SELINA... AND HER *LEAVING* HURT ME *DEEPLY.*

BUT SHE *DID* LEAVE--BY HER *OWN CHOICE*-- AND NOW *VICKI* AND I HAVE--

EH?

VVRRROOOMM

"SELINA!"

GOTHAM GENERAL HOSPITAL: NOON.

HI, STRANGER. HAVE A GOOD REST?

BRUCE...

I FEEL LIKE I'VE SLEPT FOR HOURS.

MAKE THAT TWO DAYS.

TWO--? BRUCE, THIS IS A HOSPITAL...

WHAT HAPPENED TO ME?

A MILD CONCUSSION... BUT YOU'RE GOING TO BE FINE.

REMEMBER ANYTHING ABOUT THE CRASH--?

ALL I REMEMBER IS DREAMING I WAS ASLEEP... AND THAT YOU WERE WITH ME, BESIDE ME...

YOU WERE, WEREN'T YOU?

BRUCE NODS, BUT VICKI IS ALREADY ASLEEP ONCE MORE...

OUTSIDE IN THE HALL, THREE FRIENDS STAND WAITING ANXIOUSLY, AND EACH RELAXES VISIBLY AT THE SIGHT OF WAYNE'S EXPRESSION...

SHE'S ALL RIGHT-- THANK GOD.

ANY WORD ABOUT CATWOMAN?

WE DID AS YOU ASKED, BRUCE. BARD AND GORDON, INVESTIGATIONS HAS HANDLED THIS ALONE, NOT REPORTING IT TO THE POLICE.

WE'VE HAD HER APARTMENT STAKED OUT FOR FORTY-EIGHT HOURS... BARBARA IS THERE NOW...

...BUT SO FAR SELINA HASN'T APPEARED.

ALL THAT MEANS IS SHE HASN'T GONE IN OR OUT.

SHE COULD BE HOLED UP INSIDE.

BRUCE, I HAVE TO KNOW--

JUST WHAT ARE YOU PLANNING?

YOU'RE WASTING YOUR TIME, JASON.

TAKE IT FROM AN OLD EX-COMMISSIONER OF POLICE--BRUCE CAN STONEWALL WITH THE BEST OF THEM.

8

SORRY, DICK, BUT THIS IS *PERSONAL.*

BESIDES, YOU'VE BEEN HELPING ME TOO *MUCH* LATELY-- YOU EVEN TOOK MY PLACE *TWICE* IN THE PAST FEW WEEKS *--

--AND THAT CAN'T BE DOING YOUR RELATIONSHIP WITH THE *TITANS* ANY GOOD.

WRONG.

BRUCE, MY FIRST DUTY AS *ROBIN* IS TO *YOU*--

* SEE OUR PAST TWO ISSUES. --*Len.*

YOUR *FIRST* DUTY IS TO *YOURSELF.*

BE RESPONSIBLE FOR YOURSELF, DICK--

-- AND ALL THE REST WILL FOLLOW.

THAT'S SOMETHING *CATWOMAN* MUST COME TO UNDERSTAND.

SHE'S TRIED TO MAKE *VICKI* AND ME RESPONSIBLE FOR *HER* HAPPINESS.

LIFE DOESN'T *WORK* THAT WAY.

C'MON, BRUCE, YOU *KNOW* BETTER.

WE *ARE* RESPONSIBLE FOR EACH OTHER.

THAT'S PART OF BEING *HUMAN...* ISN'T IT?

10

YOU *RAISED* ME... TAUGHT ME HOW TO BE A *MAN*... TOOK RESPONSIBILITY FOR MY *LIFE*.

AND IT WAS *GOOD* FOR YOU, TOO, BRUCE.

I THINK--HAVING ME UNDERFOOT ALL THOSE YEARS-- KEPT YOU *SANE*.

TIMES CHANGE, DICK... *PEOPLE* CHANGE.

ANYWAY AS I SAID--

THIS ONE IS *PERSONAL.*

I'VE NEVER SEEN THE MASTER QUITE SO *COLD*, YOUNG SIR.

EXCEPT WHEN HE SPEAKS OF *JOE CHILL*--

--THE MAN WHO MURDERED HIS *PARENTS.* *WHEW!!*

SELINA AND I HAVE NEVER *GOTTEN ALONG,* BUT SHE'S NOT *THAT BAD*-- NOT *ANYMORE.*

SOMETHING'S *HAPPENING* TO BRUCE, ALFRED.

IT'S BEEN SETTLING IN FOR A LONG TIME.

AND IT'S NOT *GOOD.*

SELINA KYLE'S APARTMENT BUILDING!

NIGHT.

SWISSHH

KLINK

11

197

SILENCE.

IN THE APARTMENT, A FAINT RUSTLE... A SHADOW PACING.

SNIK

SELINA?

GROWWR

HISSSSS

SELINA'S PANTHER!

ITS EYES-- WILD, VICIOUS!

GOING TO LEAP--

12

BILLS ARE LIKE A *DIARY*.

THEY CAN REVEAL A PERSON'S *SECRETS*-- HIS AMBITIONS, HIS FRUSTRATIONS--

C **CATAMONT WAREHOUSE** INC.

NOTICE: Selina Kyle *TENANT*

ACCORDING TO AGREED UPON TERMS, RENT PAID IN FULL ON SIX MONTHS LEASE.

NEW BALANCE 00.00

--HIS *PAST*, AND HIS *FUTURE*.

JACKPOT.

GOTHAM CITY HALL...

I'M GOING TO *ENJOY* THIS.

I HAVEN'T HAD A GOOD PIPE IN *SIX MONTHS*, SINCE *HILL* UP THERE *FIRED* ME...

THEY ALL TASTED *BITTER*, SOMEHOW.

BUT I'LL TELL YOU SOMETHING, BARBARA... JASON...

...*THIS* ONE TASTES SWEET.

DAD'S FINALLY *HIMSELF* AGAIN, JASON.

THANK YOU.

JIM GORDON'S A TOUGH OLD *COP*, BARBARA.

ALL HE NEEDED WAS A *NUDGE*--

--AND A *CAUSE*.

16

DO YOU THINK WE'RE FINALLY *RID* OF RUPERT THORNE NOW, JASON?

HE WON'T COME *CRAWLING BACK* AGAIN -- LIKE LAST TIME...?

BARBARA, THORNE *KILLED A MAN* BEFORE *WITNESSES* --

AND NOT JUST *ANYONE*... HE SHOT HIS OWN HAND-PICKED *POLICE COMMISSIONER!*

NOT ONLY *THAT* --

-- YOUR FATHER AND I HAVE FOUND STRONG EVIDENCE LINKING *THORNE* TO HAMILTON HILL'S MAYORAL CAMPAIGN.

WE HAD THE BATMAN'S HELP, BUT IT WAS *JIM GORDON* WHO KEPT PUSHING TILL WE LEARNED THE *TRUTH.*

NOW *HILL* WANTS TO SEE HIM...

WHAT I WOULDN'T *GIVE* TO SEE *THAT* --!

CITY HALL, THIRD FLOOR...

HELLO, HAMILTON. YOU LOOK *WORRIED.*

MORE BAD NEWS?

I'M *STILL* THE MAYOR, GORDON.

IF YOU DON'T RESPECT *ME,* RESPECT THE *OFFICE.*

YES, I'VE HAD BAD NEWS...

LOOK AT *THIS.*

I CAN'T SAY I'M *SURPRISED.*

WHEN WORD GOT OUT THAT *THORNE* HAD A PART IN YOUR *CAMPAIGN,* THIS WAS *BOUND* TO HAPPEN.

PETITION TO RECALL

DAMN IT, MAN, A *RECALL* ELECTION WILL TEAR THIS CITY APART. I NEED TO *DEFUSE* IT -- HERE AND *NOW!*

I'M HEADING INTO A ROUND OF *SENSITIVE* UNION NEGOTIATIONS -- THERE'S A NEW *BOND ISSUE* THE CITY'S OFFERING TO THE MAJOR *BANKS* --

-- AND I'M *PERSONALLY* SPEARHEADING THE DRIVE AGAINST THIS *NEW FEDERALISM* INSANITY!

SO?

17

From THE BATMAN'S CRIME-FILE

COBBLEPOT, OSWALD CHESTERFIELD
Alias **THE PENGUIN**.

SUBJECT OF THIS FILE:

The PENGUIN'S

THE PENGUIN MUST ALWAYS BE CONSIDERED ARMED AND WITH MEANS OF ESCAPE AT HAND SO LONG AS HE HAS ONE OF HIS TRICK **UMBRELLAS** HANDY.

BANG!

IN HIS VERY FIRST APPEARANCE (*DETECTIVE COMICS* #58; DEC., 1941), THE *PENGUIN*, MASQUERADING UNDER THE NAME OF *MR. BONIFACE*, USED UMBRELLAS WHICH SHOT *BULLETS*, *KNOCKOUT GAS* AND *ACID*!

IN *BATMAN* #14 (DEC., 1942), THE *FOWL FELON* HAD AN INSIDE-OUT UMBRELLA, WITH NEEDLE-SHARP, POISON STAYS!

IN THAT SAME STORY, "BARGAINS IN BANDITRY," *BATMAN* AND *ROBIN* CRASHED THE *PENGUIN'S* NEST ...ONLY TO FIND THE *UMBRELLA-RUG* WAS A TRAP, RIGGED TO CATCH THEM AND PUT THEM TO SLEEP WITH GAS!

24

UNIQUE UMBRELLAS!

"THE THREE ECCENTRICS" (*BATMAN* #21; FEB.–MAR., 1944) GAVE THE *BEAKED BADMAN* A CHANCE TO USE HIS *REAR-VIEW UMBRELLA* TO SPOT THE PURSUING MANHUNTER!

TWO UMBRELLAS WERE INTRODUCED IN "CRIME ON THE WING" (*BATMAN* #33; FEB.–MAR., 1946). ONE TURNED UMBRELLA SILK AND RIBS INTO A WEB TO CATCH *BATMAN*...

...WHILE THE OTHER, DROPPED "ACCIDENTALLY," WAS A BOOBY-TRAP WHICH SHOT GAS AT *BATMAN* WHEN HE TRIED TO USE IT ON THE *PENGUIN!*

TRANSPORTATION? "THE PENGUIN'S NEST" (*BATMAN* #36; AUG.–SEPT., 1946) INCLUDED A *PARACHUTE-UMBRELLA* CONCEALED IN A HAT, AND A *POGO-STICK-UMBRELLA!*

AND THIS ONE FROM "THE PENGUIN ON PAROLE" (*BATMAN* #38; DEC.–JAN., 1946) WAS A COMBINATION *HELICOPTER* AND *TEAR-GAS GUN!*

A MORE MODERN ESCAPE-GIMMICK WAS THE *ROCKET-UMBRELLA* USED IN "PARTNERS IN PLUNDER" (*BATMAN* #169; FEB., 1965)!

HERE WE HAVE THE ULTIMATE UMBRELLA... A ROBOT-CONTROLLED MODEL THAT DID THE ROBBING FOR ITS CREATOR, WHILE HE STAYED IN HIS LAIR!

"THE PENGUIN TAKES A FLYER-- INTO THE FUTURE" (*BATMAN* #190; MARCH, 1967).

25

THE *PAROLE BOARD* THANKS YOU FOR YOUR *IMPASSIONED* PRESENTATION, MR. COBBLEPOT-- YOU'LL BE INFORMED OF OUR DECISION SHORTLY.

THANK YOU. I SINCERELY THANK YOU.

"SEND IN THE NEXT WITNESS, GUARD--"

AWK! WHAT ARE *YOU* DOING HERE?

I'VE COME TO OFFER MY INSIGHTS ON YOUR *CHARACTER* TO THE BOARD MEMBERS.

BUT MY DEAR FELLOW, I'VE *CHANGED*-- WHERE ONCE A FOUL HEART ROOSTED, NOW BEATS A VIRTUAL *VALENTINE* OF VIRTUE!

SPARE THE BIRDSEED FOR THE *PIGEONS*, PENGUIN--

B-BUT...

COME ALONG, PENGUIN--YOU'RE NOT A FREE MAN YET!

2

AT THE REQUEST OF COMMISSIONER GORDON, WE'VE GRANTED YOUR REQUEST TO BE *HEARD* IN THE CASE OF *OSWALD C. COBBLEPOT--*

ALIAS THE *PENGUIN*--YES. AND THANK YOU FOR HEARING ME. NOW--

YOU SHOULD KNOW AT THE OUTSET THAT SEVERAL BOARD MEMBERS HAVE FILED *PROTESTS* AGAINST YOUR APPEARANCE HERE--

"*PROTESTS?* WHY, WITH ALL DUE RESPECT, NO ONE KNOWS THAT *SCHEMING LITTLE VULTURE* BETTER THAN..."

NO ONE DOUBTS YOUR FAMILIARITY WITH MR. COBBLEPOT-- OR YOUR *BIAS*--

AREN'T YOU PEOPLE FORGETTING THE *FACTS?* THE PENGUIN IS NOT ONLY A MASTER *THIEF*, HE'S A CON MAN--DON'T LET HIM *FOOL* YOU!

"WHY, HE'S BEEN IN AND OUT OF GOTHAM PRISON FOR *TWENTY YEARS*-- THAT CUSTOM PRISONER'S UNIFORM HE'S ALLOWED TO WEAR IS PRACTICALLY AN ANTIQUE.'"

3

IF IT WERE UP TO ME...

BUT IT ISN'T. YOU HAVE *NO OFFICIAL* AUTHORITY. THERE ARE, IN FACT, THOSE OF US WHO VIEW YOU AS A *VIGILANTE*--

I PERSONALLY FIND IT *LUDICROUS* THAT WE HAVE EVEN *ALLOWED* THE PRESENCE OF A *MASKED OUTLAW* TO SULLY THE DIGNITY OF THESE PROCEEDINGS...

SLAM

THAT BAD, HUH?

WANT TO TALK ABOUT IT?

ACTION IS WHAT'S CALLED FOR. TALKING'S FOR THE BIRDS.

BUT, GEE-- WHAT IF THE PENGUIN'S *REALLY* REFORMED? SHOULDN'T WE GIVE HIM THE BENEFIT OF...

"ROBIN, LESSON FOR THE DAY: LEOPARDS DON'T CHANGE THEIR SPOTS; AND PENGUINS DON'T CHANGE THEIR *PLUMAGE*--"

OKAY, PENGIE-- YOU'RE *OUTA* HERE! FLY THE COOP, ALREADY!

4

AND SOON A DAPPER PAROLEE IS MAKING A SOCIAL CALL --

MY HEART FLUTTERS LIKE A *FLEDGLING!* COURAGE, PENGUIN, COURAGE....

OSWALD! YOUR PAROLE CAME THROUGH! WHY DIDN'T YOU SEND WORD?!?

NO CARRIER PIGEONS ALLOWED IN STIR, MY DEAR.

DOVINA, MY DEAR-- YOUR PICTURE DIDN'T DO YOU *JUSTICE!*

OH--OSWALD-- HOW WELL I FEEL I *KNOW* YOU, FROM YOUR LOVELY LETTERS--

IMAGINE--WHAT BEGAN AS A SIMPLE EXCHANGE OF MISSIVES, HATCHED IN THE PERSONAL COLUMN OF THE *ORNITHOLOGICAL NEWS*....

HAS SPREAD ITS WINGS INTO... DARE I *SAY* IT? A ROMANCE IN *FULL FLIGHT!*

SAY IT, MY LOVE! SAY IT!

AFTER A PROPER *COURTSHIP*, DEAR DOVINA, YOU MAY EXPECT A PROPOSAL OF MATRIMONY...

AND YOU MAY EXPECT AN AFFIRMATIVE RESPONSE....ON ONE CONDITION--

5

BATMAN! YOU'RE NOTHING IF NOT *PROMPT*--

WE WERE ON PATROL NEARBY. WHAT'S THE PENGUIN *DONE?*

WHY, *NOTHING*--THIS IS JUST A *ROUTINE* MATTER... RASH OF LIQUOR STORE ROBBERIES...

CRIME IS CRIME. BATMAN AND ROBIN GO TO WORK...

LIQUOR

SMALL-TIMERS.

EIGHT LIQUOR STORES IN ONE NIGHT ISN'T SO *SMALL-TIME.* ESPECIALLY NOT TO THE EIGHT LIQUOR STORE OWNERS.

BATMAN, CUT ME A *DEAL* AND I'LL CLUE YA IN ON SOMETHING *BIG*--

I'LL CUT YOU A DEAL. *SPILL* AND YOU KEEP YOUR TEETH.

7

HEY, ISN'T IT A LITTLE *EARLY* FOR YOU TO BE UP? IT'S NINE O'CLOCK IN THE *MORNING!*

I HAVEN'T BEEN *HOME* YET.

I HEARD YOU NABBED THOSE *LIQUOR STORE* HEISTERS. THANKS FOR THE PROMPT SERVICE.

FINE. NOW GIVE *ME* SOME. WHAT'S THE PENGUIN UP TO? I HEAR HE'S PUT THE WORD OUT FOR HIS OLD *CRONIES* TO HOOK UP WITH HIM...

WE HAVEN'T HEARD THAT. FAR AS WE KNOW, PENGUIN'S GONE *STRAIGHT*--HE'S OPENED AN *UMBRELLA* FACTORY.

OH, *PLEASE!*

"LOOK," GORDON SAYS, "WE'VE BEEN WATCHING MR. COBBLEPOT LIKE A *HAWK*--HE SHUTTLES FROM HIS LOVE NEST WITH MISS DOVINA PARTRIDGE, TO THIS FACTORY HE'S OPENING, AND BACK AGAIN... THAT'S THE *WHOLE STORY!*"

GOTHAM UMBRELLA WORKS

PECK

"WHAT'S THE STORY ON HIS GIRL-FRIEND?" BATMAN ASKS. "GOOD FAMILY BACKGROUND--VERY UPRIGHT LADY," SAYS GORDON. "SHE AND PENGUIN FELL IN LOVE BY MAIL--"

WELL, I MUST *FLY*, MY LOVE! AN HONEST DOLLAR CALLS!

⑧

OH, DEAR-- OSWALD MUST'VE *FORGOTTEN* SOMETHING!

OSWAL... OH. IT'S YOU.

MAY I COME IN?

CERTAINLY. I'VE WANTED A *WORD* WITH YOU FOR *SOME TIME.*

SEE HERE, YOUNG MAN--MY OSWALD IS *REFORMED.* HE NEVER STOLE FOR THE MONEY-- AFTER ALL, HE INHERITED A FAMILY *FORTUNE!* HE ONLY WANTED ATTENTION-- APPROVAL--

"THE PRISON PSYCHIATRIST SAID OSWALD'S PENCHANT FOR COLLECTING WAS A SIMPLE *ANAL RETENTIVE TENDENCY* WHICH CAN BE OVERCOME BY *THERAPY AND LOVE!*"

MISS PARTRIDGE--I PROMISE YOU I WILL *NOT* PERSECUTE "OSWALD." IF HE AND I TANGLE, REST ASSURED HE WILL HAVE *DESERVED* MY ATTENTION--

"WHAT YOU REFER TO AS 'COLLECTING,' I REFER TO AS 'STEALING.' AND IF HE BEGINS 'COLLECTING' AGAIN, I'LL CAGE HIM AGAIN."

RELLA WORKS

GOOD DAY, GENTLEMEN.

HIYA, BOSS.

YOU STRIKE ME AS AN *HONORABLE* INDIVIDUAL. I WILL TRUST YOUR JUDGMENT.

OH, OSWALD... OSWALD... DO BE A GOOD BOY...

NIGHT FOLLOWS DAY. BATMAN FOLLOWS PENGUIN.

WHAT'S GOING ON DOWN THERE?

I DON'T KNOW.

GOTHAM UMBRELLA WORKS

"BUT IF THAT UMBRELLA FACTORY IS FOR REAL, I'LL EAT MY CAPE--"

10

223

CHIRP! CHIRP! CHIRP! CHIRP! CHIRP!

IT'S SOME KIND OF ALARM!

STAY DOWN HERE AND KEEP AN EYE OUT--I'M GOING UP AFTER HIM--

CHIRP! CHIRP! CHIRP! CHIRP! CHIR

COPS!

JJJJJJ

WE GOTTA SPLIT--

PENGUIN! I KNOW YOU'RE UP HERE--

INDEED I AM--AND WITH MY TRUSTY BUMBERSHOOTER, .357 MAG!

I HOPE YOU'RE SATISFIED. YOU'VE RUINED ME. MY ONE TRUE LOVE WILL BE FOREVER LOST TO ME--

THEN YOU SHOULDN'T HAVE GOTTEN BACK INTO CRIME--

13

AH, BUT I *DIDN'T* DEAR FELLOW. THIS BUSINESS IS *QUITE* LEGITIMATE--

"I HAVE BROUGHT MY MASTERY OF THE UMBRELLA-MAKER'S ART TO ASSEMBLY-LINE PRODUCTION--"

GOTHAM UMBRELLA WORKS

THEN WHY THE HEAVILY ARMED *GUARDS?*

TO KEEP PRYING EYES *OUT*--

OF *COMPETITORS?*

NO! WAK! WAK! OF *YOURS*... AND THE *POLICE!*

YOU SEE, MOST OF MY EMPLOYEES ARE LIKE ME-- EX-CONS WHO CAN'T GET A BREAK! AND FLOCKING TOGETHER WITH SUCH BIRDS OF A FEATHER PUTS ME...

AH, I SEE THAT MY BOYS HAVE FOR THE MOST PART *FLOWN.* YOU MAY TAKE ME IN NOW.... AND THIS IS *NOT* A GUN. MERELY AN *UMBRELLA*-- ALBEIT OF AN EXTREMELY HIGH QUALITY.

IN VIOLATION OF PAROLE.

14

AND THAT, LADIES AND GENTLEMEN, IS MY STORY--

SYMPATHETIC AS WE MIGHT BE TO MR. COBBLEPOT'S GOOD INTENTIONS, HE IS STILL IN VIOLATION OF HIS PAROLE.

NEXT CAGE.

SLAM

THAT BAD, HUH?

"POOR PENGUIN SITS IN HIS CELL BROODING OVER HIS LOST LOVE," SAYS THE BATMAN, "AND IT'S MY FAULT--"

BUT MAYBE I CAN DO SOMETHING TO MAKE UP FOR LAYING THIS PARTICULAR EGG--

15

SOON--

YOU GOT A VISITOR, PENGUIN--

SO THEN YOU WILL MARRY ME? YOU RECOGNIZE THAT MY HEART WAS IN THE RIGHT PLACE? HOW...?

A LITTLE BAT TOLD ME.

THE END

"EERIE"

QUICK FOOTSTERS STRIKE THE CAMPUS ROAD LIKE DRUMBEATS.

THESE DRUMBEATS ARE SOON DROWNED OUT BY A FASTER, MORE FRENZIED CADENCE--

G-2745

--THE SOUND OF BEATING WINGS!

THE DRUMMING IS ACCOMPANIED BY SHRILL CRIES--

--CRIES THAT SEEM TO SAY, "KILL...KILL...

--KILL!"

JOEY CAVALIERI
WRITER
KLAUS JANSON
ARTIST / COLORIST
JOHN COSTANZA
letterer
DENNIS O'NEIL
EDITOR

A REMARKABLE BIRD OF PREY, THE FALCON.

THE TYPICAL PEREGRINE CAN DIVE AT A SPEED OF EIGHTY MILES AN HOUR--

IMAGINE THE SPEED, THEN, OF A FALCON *TWICE* NORMAL SIZE--

--A BIRD IN SHORT--

-- THAT IS A *MONSTER!*

THE BIRD'S GETTING AWAY!

MEET ME BELOW!

IMPORTANT? *I'LL* TELL YOU WHAT'S IMPORTANT.

IF I HAD TO CHOOSE BETWEEN THAT BOX AND YOU--

--*YOU'D* HAVE TO GO!

THESE COMPUTER DISKS HOLD THE NOTES TO THE GRAND AND GLORIOUS BREEDING EXPERIMENT THAT PRODUCED THESE PRIZE PEREGRINES!

NEVER BEFORE HAVE FALCONS OF SUCH SIZE BE--

IDIOTS! CRETINS!

GET THIS MAMMOTH MONSTROSITY AWAY FROM ME!

SORRY, BOSS. THE BIRD MUST'VE WANTED THAT BOX AS MUCH AS *YOU* DO.

WE PRETTY MUCH GOT A HANDLE ON 'EM NOW.

SEE THAT *YOU* DO.

WE LOST *ONE* FALCON THROUGH YOUR INCOMPETENCE. WE CAN'T AFFORD *ANOTHER* SUCH LOSS.

DR. BAIRD HERE WOULDN'T LIKE IT...

BUT I'M SURE THERE'S A LOT HE WOULDN'T LIKE... SINCE HE'S BECOME A PRECIOUS *PART* OF OUR PLUNDER... HMMMM?

WH-WHAT... WHAT DO YOU MEAN?

⑦

WHAT I MEAN IS, THEY'RE VERY VALUABLE BIRDS... BECAUSE THEY'RE *EXPERIMENTAL*... *UNIQUE*...

BUT THEY WON'T *REMAIN SO*, IF YOU CAN *BREED* MORE *LIKE* THEM! THAT'S WHY WE'RE ABSCONDING WITH YOUR *LAB NOTES*...

AND *YOU* AS WELL!

NO! NO!

ALL MY WORK!

I CAN'T LET THIS HAPPEN!

I DON'T RECALL THROWING IT OPEN TO A VOTE.

EGG ON YOUR FACE? WEAR IT AND *LIKE* IT.

YOU'RE NOT GOING TO BE MUCH TROUBLE. WE KNOW YOU BETTER THAN YOU KNOW YOURSELF. EVEN IF YOU *COULD* OFFER RESISTANCE, YOU *WON'T*... FOR FEAR WE'LL HARM YOUR *FALCONS*.

I REMEMBER READING OF AN *ORIENTAL* NOBLEMAN WHO WEPT *OPENLY* WHEN HE DISCOVERED HIS PRIZE FALCON HAD DIED.

HE CURSED THE SKIES THAT THE GODS HAD NOT TAKEN HIS ONLY SON *INSTEAD*.

8

NO, MY FRIEND.

I'M WAGERING YOU'LL REMAIN *VERY* COOPERATIVE!

COOPERATIVE *INDEED*... WITH HIS *TESTIMONY* AT YOUR *TRIAL.*

DRAT! THIS WILL BE A WASTE OF PRECIOUS TIME!

NOW WE'LL HIT TRAFFIC FROM THE *RALLY* ON THE WAY BACK!

YOU'LL BE LUCKY IF THAT'S ALL YOU HIT.

THE BOSS IS ALLERGIC TO BATMAN. BREAKS OUT IN A RASH WHENEVER HE'S AROUND.

SO DON'T LET 'IM GET TOO *CLOSE*, HEAR?

NORMALLY, THESE HOOKSTICKS ARE USED TO BRING FALCONS DOWN FROM TREES BY LOOPING THE LEATHER THONGS ON THEIR LEGS...

9

...BUT I CAN FIND ANOTHER USE FOR IT!

...FOR THE TIME BEING...

...IT WILL MAKE AN IMPROMPTU VERSION...

...OF A BO STICK!

WELL DONE, BATMAN. TRULY ENTERTAINING. MORE EXCITING THAN FOURTH OF JULY FIREWORKS!

BUT IF YOU TRULY WANT TO SEE A PYRO-TECHNICAL DISPLAY--

CHIK!

--TAKE ONE STEP CLOSER! I PROMISE A BURST OF SCARLET BRILLIANCE NO ROMAN CANDLE CAN MATCH!

LET'S NOT SAY "GOODBYE", BATMAN... LET'S MERELY SAY...

..."UNTIL WE MEET AGAIN!"

10

WHEN YOU GET SECRETIVE LIKE THIS, IT MAKES ME *CRAZY*.

I MEAN, IF YOU HAVE EVEN THE *SLIGHTEST* IDEA WHERE THE PENGUIN COULD HAVE TAKEN THOSE BIRDS, I WISH YOU'D LET ME IN ON IT!

TO ME, IT'S LIKE A VARIATION OF AN OLD JOKE. "WHERE DOES A TWENTY-FIVE POUND FALCON GO TO EAT?"

"ANYWHERE HE WANTS TO!" GET IT?

DO *YOU* GET IT? THAT'S THE *POINT*. WHERE *WOULD* THOSE FALCONS *WANT* TO GO?

I THINK I'VE LEARNED ENOUGH ABOUT THEIR NESTING HABITS, AND THEIR NEEDS AS BIRDS OF PREY, TO BE NEARLY *CERTAIN*.

EVEN IF YOU *DO*, I DON'T KNOW WHAT YOU WANT WITH THESE BIRD CALLS.

I'M NOT SURE I'D WANT THOSE THINGS TO BE TOO TERRIBLY *ATTRACTED* TO ME. IF I HAD TO SHARE A *NEST* WITH A BIRD LIKE THAT--

SKREEK SKREEK

237

"--I'D HOPE IT WAS A PRETTY ROOMY ONE!"

A VERY CLEVER BIT OF WORK!

TELL ME, HAVE WE HEARD ANYTHING SINCE OUR RANSOM DEMAND?

NOTHING YET. IT STILL TAKES TIME TO HEAR FROM HALFWAY 'ROUND THE WORLD!

WHAT MAKES YOU THINK YOU'LL COLLECT?

YOU MUST BE JOKING-- THAT ARAB SHEIK FRIEND OF YOURS IS MADE OF MONEY!

AFTER ALL, HE HAD NOTHING BETTER TO DO WITH HIS DOUGH THAN TO ENDOW GOTHAM UNIVERSITY --AND YOU--WITH ENOUGH FOR YOU TO GENETICALLY PRODUCE THAT PACK OF PRODIGIOUS PEREGRINES!

SO HE'S GOT EIGHT HOURS TO COME ACROSS-- OR HIS EXPERIMENTAL GIFT TO THE SPORT OF FALCONRY WILL BE WIPED OFF THE DISKS... AND THE LANDSCAPE...

...AND YOU ALONG WITH IT!

NOT TO MENTION A WONDERFULLY UNEXPECTED DIVIDEND ON MY INVESTMENT--

12

ANOTHER MINUTE AND--

--THE PENGUIN--

--WILL FIND HIMSELF--

--AN ENDANGERED SPECIES!

OH, NO! I SHOULD HAVE EXPECTED AS MUCH FROM HIM!

IT'S--

SPRANNNG!

--A DECOY!

CUCKOO! CUCKOO!

THE ALARM!

THE BAT'S TAKEN THE BAIT!

14

WELCOME, BATMAN... TO MY MAKESHIFT TEMPLE TO THE GOD *RA*, PERSONIFIED BY THE SACRED *FALCON.*

HERE, AS IS WRITTEN IN THE EGYPTIAN CURSE--

"--DEATH WILL COME ON SWIFT WINGS!"

MANAGED TO HIDE HIS *TABLE KNIFE...* ANOTHER FEW SECONDS, NOW...

...JUST AS LONG AS THEY KEEP WATCHING OUT THE WINDOW... AND NOT AT ME!

YOU HAVEN'T A *CHANCE,* BATMAN!

CHANCE FAVORS THE PREPARED... AND I CAME PREPARED!

I BROUGHT THIS FROM THE *BAT CAVE*...FIGURING I'D EVENTUALLY HAVE TO FEND OFF THE FALCONS!

⑮

IT'S WORKING JUST AS I HOPED IT WOULD!

SKREEEEEEE

I PRE-RECORDED THE CRY OF A FALCON THAT SIGNALS "DANGER." IT'S THEIR OWN CODE TO FLEE FROM AN ATTACKER... THE BIRDS ARE NOW ACTUALLY AFRAID OF ME!

THE PENGUIN THOUGHT HE WAS FUNNY TRIPPING ME UP. WE'LL SEE WHO LAUGHS THIS TIME.

HE DOESN'T SEEM SO INTERESTED IN ME AT PRESENT... WHICH GIVES ME THE OPPORTUNITY TO BORROW...

...THIS FALCON LURE. FALCONERS USE THEM TO ATTRACT THE BIRDS... IT'S MADE TO LOOK LIKE THE FALCONS' QUARRY!

NOW TO GET MY FILE DISKS!

THOSE FALCONS HAVE TURNED CHICKEN!

IT'S THE NOISEMAKER HE BROUGHT ALONG!

GET IT AWAY FROM HIM! GET IT!

FOR PITY'S SAKE, MOVE FASTER! THAT'S BATMAN IN THAT BIRDCAGE, NOT SOME BUDGIE!

EEEEE

THE GOOD DOCTOR HAS A PLAN IN MIND, I SEE--

SKREE

16

--A PLAN I CAN MAKE SUCCEED!

NO! *NO!!*

THOSE BIRDS ARE OUR *FORTUNE!* DON'T LET THEM GET AWAY!

YOU NEEDN'T WORRY, PENGUIN! THEY WON'T BE GOING VERY *FAR!*

FIRST THEY'RE ATTRACTED TO THE *BRIGHT BOX--*

17

AND I CERTAINLY HOPE TO *RETURN* THE FAVOR AT THE EARLIEST OPPORTUNITY!

SO WHEN AND UNTIL THAT DAY PRESENTS ITSELF, I BELIEVE I'LL SIMPLY BID YOU A CIVIL--

--Adieu.

NOT A VERY *TRUSTING* INDIVIDUAL, ARE YOU?

21

THE FOLLOWING MORNING...

THE "SUPER HERO" IS AN AFFRONT TO THE COMMON MAN...

...AN *INSULT* TO THE TALENTS AND CAPABILITIES OF THE COMMON MAN TO COPE WITH THE WORLD AS HE FINDS IT!

TOO LONG HAS THE COMMON MAN BEEN HELD BACK BY THE PRESENCE OF THESE "SUPERMEN"... TOO LONG HAVE THEIR EFFORTS BEEN STIFLED BY THOSE WHO WOULD BETTER THEMSELVES AT *OUR* EXPENSE!

ELIMINATE THE SUPER HERO... AND WITNESS THE *TRIUMPH* OF THE COMMON MAN!

GODFREY'S RALLY AT GOTHAM UNIVERSITY WAS WELL-ATTENDED. CAMPUS SECURITY CLAIMED ALMOST A THOUSAND STUDENTS HEARD GODFREY SPEAK...

AND SOME WITNESSES CLAIM EVEN BATMAN AND ROBIN WERE ON HAND AS WELL.

YOU THINK HE'S *RIGHT*, BRUCE?

I THINK HE'S RIGHT ON AT LEAST ONE IMPORTANT POINT...

LAST NIGHT, THAT BAIRD FELLOW DID A FINE JOB OF HOLDING HIS OWN AGAINST THE PENGUIN...

I THINK THE *"TRIUMPH OF THE COMMON MAN"* IS ASSURED...

...WHETHER OR NOT THERE'S A BATMAN TO HELP HIM.

The End

22

Batman probably has the most interesting, colorful and deadly rogues gallery in comic books (that honor in comic *strips* reserved for *Dick Tracy*). In our first volume most of Batman's best-known foes appeared, however briefly. The Joker, Catwoman, Penguin, Two-Face, et al., all made an appearance; yet it was felt that since the Joker was indeed Batman's greatest foe and inspiration for an armload of classic confrontations, the Clown Prince of Crime deserved his own volume.

In reviewing material for this volume, it was apparent that although Batman has many memorable enemies, after fifty years, the quality of their stories did not always stand up well to the test of time. As a result, with a nod toward the summer, 1992 release of *Batman Returns*, this volume would concentrate on meetings between the Caped Crusader and the Penguin and Catwoman.

To the casual reader, the various interpretations of the characters may seem quite inconsistent from beginning to end; this section of the volume will attempt to sort out some of that continuity. While the Penguin went from deadly to comical-but-deadly to just-plain-deadly, the Catwoman has been many things.

In the beginning, the Catwoman was a beautiful cat burglar, styled after screen star Hedy Lamarr. In short order, though, as costumed characters became the norm in comics, she donned a cat's head mask and plagued the Dynamic Duo. By the mid-1940s, her familiar purple-and-green outfit had been designed, and was used right through the 1950s. While that in itself is not necessarily confusing, it should be noted that Selina Kyle's personality has been under constant revision. While she seemed your basic female criminal through the 1940s, it turns out that she was a normal young woman, who had been injured in an airplane accident and survived sans her memory. Lost and aimless, she turned to crime and, for a decade, plagued Gotham City as the Cat, later Catwoman. Ultimately, another blow to the head restored her memory and she foreswore crime. That story, presented in BATMAN #62 (1950), was a very early attempt at characterization and continuity, something virtually unheard of in comics at that time. She appeared infrequently from 1950 to 1952, helping Batman when circumstances demanded it (such as her brother's sudden arrival as a cos- tumed criminal), but returning to crime in the story presented here, "The Crimes of the Catwoman."

During her formative appearances in BATMAN and DETECTIVE COMICS, Catwoman displayed an attraction for Batman that fans recall most about her. As a result, she was often willing to spare Batman or Robin's life—a perfect example of which is contained in our first volume, "The Jungle Cat-Queen." Creator Bob Kane admits today that Catwoman was invented for the originality of having a female antagonist and to play off that attraction between opposites. Very rarely did either woman were allowed to finally proclaim their love and marry in the memorable "The Autobiography of Bruce Wayne," reprinted in volume one. A side note to fans: this union produced a daughter, Helena Wayne, who became the costumed crimefighter called The Huntress when her mother was killed. That origin story was the final appearance of that original Catwoman.

Confusing enough was what became of the modern-day Catwoman. In the 1970s she was just a costumed foe relying on cat-crimes, and few of her stories were of any particular note. One, though, did have Batman stop and wonder for a few panels about the two women in his life, Catwoman and Talia, daughter of Rā's al Ghūl. Both were on the "wrong" side of the law and he couldn't fathom his attraction to them—or what to do about it.

In the early 1980s, Selina Kyle returned, swearing she had reformed and, with Bruce Wayne's help, became a legitimate business-woman. She even began romancing Wayne while occasionally fighting side by side with The Batman. This led to some very memorable subplots from writers Len Wein and Marv Wolfman, but they did not lead to very strong Catwoman-oriented stories for this collection. This interpretation of the character did lead to a short-lived series of backup features starring the adventurous Catwoman. The first two installments are presented here, representing the best of that run.

Frank Miller turned everyone's head when his classic THE DARK KNIGHT RETURNS burst on the comics scene in 1986. There, the story projects what happens when Bruce Wayne is 50 and is forced out of retirement one last time. Catwoman appears in the story, characterized as a hardened, embittered prostitute. This led Miller to write a brand-new origin and characterization for the Catwoman in the acclaimed BAT-MAN: YEAR ONE, from Miller and artist David Mazzucchelli. Kyle was now a thrill-seeking prostitute with a young lesbian lover who decided to don a cat-suit to go

admit their feelings for the other, but the underlying sexual tension was there.

None of the stories used on the *Batman* television series were based on comics, and therefore do not appear here, but during the first two seasons, it was quite obvious that sexy Julie Newmar and Adam West were enjoying the sexual tensions (within the limits of network standards of that time). Such tensions were heightened as a subplot in the *Batman* feature film where Adam West was paired with Lee Meriwether, a more sultry Catwoman. Such male/female byplay was abandoned altogether when Eartha Kitt assumed the skintight cat-suit in the third and final season.

Still, the television series helped spark the return of Catwoman, who was absent for far too long in the comics. During the late 1950s and early 1960s, editor Jack Schiff abandoned the costumed criminals and had the Cowled Crusader and his youthful sidekick deal with aliens and bizarre foes such as Clayface. Some of the rationale behind this was a result of the

arrival of the Comics Code Authority and the feeling that such grotesque villains as the Joker and Two-Face would be unacceptable. If they went, the entire rogues gallery would go, too. In 1967, in another then-rare incidence of continuity, an issue of DETECTIVE COMICS concluded with a jailed Selina Kyle reading a headline about Batman and Batgirl, giving her reason to break free and claim the Darknight Detective for herself. That story, of course, is in this volume.

The 1960s also gave birth to a concept that has either enchanted or baffled readers and in some ways has forced writers to abandon some of the more interesting characters of the past. Parallel worlds, Earth-1 and Earth-2, were introduced to explain whatever happened to the original super-heroes of comics' Golden Age. The two parallel worlds continued to grow until even editors and writers had their heads spinning. All was washed away during DC Comics' 50th anniversary in 1985, but before that cataclysmic event, the Golden Age Batman and Cat-

Batman one better. The media, though, painted her as an assistant to Batman, so she swore she would make people remember her as an individual. That first confrontation set the stage for a new round of sexual politics and violent battles. Since that story was a flashback to Batman's roots, it was felt the modern-day Catwoman needed to be a villain as well, and Mike W. Barr and Alan Davis obliged in a throwaway two-parter involving the Joker.

The new version of Catwoman demanded further exploration and, after a brief run in ACTION COMICS WEEKLY, Mindy Newell, J.J. Birch and Michael Bair provided the four-part miniseries entitled CATWOMAN: HER SISTER'S KEEPER. Like THE DARK KNIGHT RETURNS and BATMAN: YEAR ONE, this story remains available in trade paperback.

Only recently has this revamped Catwoman been given additional play in the comics, and so it was deemed that these stories were too fresh for inclusion in this volume. No doubt, though, with the movie Catwoman played by Michelle Pfeiffer, comics writers and artists will once again want to explore that dark relationship between the Bat and the Cat.

The Penguin's comics history is far different, with little attention paid to his roots, the character considered a comical fellow driven to crime in order to exact revenge from those who taunted him. Tim Burton, director of both *Batman* films, has stated that he found the psychological underpinnings for the Penguin to be very weak, and this is true. Only in recent years have comics writers made an attempt to deal with the Penguin in a way that makes him a credible threat to Batman.

Originally, the Penguin was portrayed as a deadly villain with a quick trigger finger, but by 1943, he was devolved into a gimmicky foe with a penchant for umbrellas and bird crimes. He has been regarded by some as Batman's second best-known foe, and that can be traced directly back to both his memorable visual appearance and

superb portrayal on the television series by Burgess Meredith. Danny DeVito's performance is expected to make everyone reconsider the Penguin, which can only help the character in the comics.

As seen in our first volume, the Penguin was played largely for comic relief. That collection reprinted his appearance from the 1940s comic strip and an early rivalry with the Joker.

The writers of the 1940s seemed to enjoy the Penguin's gimmicks, given his relatively frequent appearances in BATMAN, DETECTIVE COMICS, and even occasionally in WORLD'S FINEST COMICS. Unfortunately, except for those gimmicks, few of the stories hold up today.

Throughout his appearances, the Penguin relied on his vanity and his criminal and mechanical genius to challenge or thwart the Dynamic Duo. He was invariably defeated and ended up in prison. As the 1950s rolled on, his appearances became less frequent; he was seen in one story in 1953, not again until 1956, and then, until 1965, he was totally missing. With the development of the TV series, starting in 1965, editor Julius Schwartz cautiously reintroduced members of the rogues gallery. The Joker, of course, was first, and the Penguin soon followed.

Interestingly, Schwartz kept the costumed foes in BATMAN while DETECTIVE was reserved for non-costumed opponents, keeping to the series name. This rule was occasionally ignored when the TV series' success had the Joker making appearances very often. During the 1960s, the Penguin was limited to two appearances, both included here, and then there were none until the 1970s.

Those 1970s appearances were inconsistent, with the two best in this volume. After that, he was again a gimmicky foe with no serious attempt at characterization or justification.

In the 1980s, the Penguin appeared very seldom but writer Doug Moench, trying to make the best of the situation, included a revelation that the Penguin was actually able to withstand arctic temperatures, just like his name-

sake. Moench and artist Don Newton tried hard with the Penguin but still couldn't come up with anything substantial.

It wasn't until the late 1980s that editor Denny O'Neil felt the time had come to remedy that. Under his guidance, Joey Cavalieri reinterpreted the character in the story seen here. Then O'Neil undertook the task to further redefine the Penguin when he wrote the very first DETECTIVE COMICS ANNUAL. The Penguin was used in a deadly manner, reminiscent of those very first appearances, but since that annual was connected with two others, it could not be collected here. Since then, O'Neil has asked his writers to keep the Penguin a fearsome foe and not just a comical caricature.

The 1990s seem destined to retain the sharped-edged interpretations of both the Penguin and Catwoman. Both have been remade for today's audiences, assuring that some of these modern-day appearances will also lay claim to the title of *greatest* Batman stories.

Robert Greenberger, currently Manager-Editorial Scheduling, has been a contributing editor to DC's Greatest Stories series since its inception.

CREATING THE GREATEST

by Paul Kupperberg

ALFREDO ALCALA

Alfredo Alcala was one of the wave of Philippine artists whose work began appearing in DC Comics in the late 1960s and early 1970s. Alfredo lent his lush illustrative style to a variety of DC stories, from short stories in the company's then-popular mystery line to the universe-spanning activities of the super-hero, to the realm of the supernatural, including work on BATMAN, ARAK, HELL-BLAZER and numerous other titles. Alfredo's work has also appeared at Marvel in such titles as *Conan*.

TERRY AUSTIN

Terry Austin began his career assisting inker Dick Giordano and quickly moved on to establish himself as one of the comics field's preeminent and most popular inkers in his own right. Terry's inks have graced the work of a number of the best pencillers in comics, including Marshall Rogers on Batman in DETECTIVE COMICS and John Byrne on Marvel Comics' *X-Men*. In addition to his work as an inker, Terry has also applied his talents as a writer on Marvel's *Cloak and Dagger*.

NORM BREYFOGLE

Norm Breyfogle was quickly recognized as *the* Batman artist for the 1990s when he took over the pencilling of DETECTIVE COMICS just a few short years ago. Since then, Norm has added the inking of his own work and painting to his repertory and, in 1992, won the plum assignment of artist on DC's fourth monthly Dark Knight title, BATMAN: SHADOW OF THE BAT.

E. NELSON BRIDWELL

E. Nelson Bridwell went from being one of comics' earliest fans in the 1950s to a position as assistant to editor Mort Weisinger in 1965. Renowned for his encyclopedic knowledge of comics history, Nelson was soon serving as DC's unofficial "continuity cop" during an era when editors and writers were only just beginning to tie together DC's more than quarter century of history. In addition to his editorial duties, Nelson was also a prolific writer. His credits include a run on the Batman syndicated newspaper strip, SHAZAM!, THE INFERIOR FIVE, THE SECRET SIX, SUPER FRIENDS, and many stories for the Superman family of titles. Nelson continued writing and editing for DC until his death in 1987.

JACK BURNLEY

Jack Burnley began cartooning for the King Features Syndicate at the tender age of 14 and, throughout the 1930s, illustrated sports and other features, including short stories by Damon Runyon. Burnley began his comic book career at Hillman Publications in 1939 and soon moved over to DC, where he worked on Superman before moving on to create Starman. Jack's distinctive style was also seen on numerous covers and features throughout the 1940s, including Batman, in both the comic books and the syndicated newspaper strip. Jack left DC and the comic book industry in 1947 to return to newspaper work, working for *The San Francisco Examiner* until his retirement in 1976. Since 1981, Jack Burnley has lived in Virginia.

JOEY CAVALIERI

Joey Cavalieri began in comics as an editor in DC's Special Projects Group and was soon scripting such features as Green Arrow, The Huntress, and Batman. He also edited LOONEY TUNES and TINY TOONS magazines, and is currently an editor at Marvel Comics.

MAX ALLAN COLLINS

Max Allan Collins is the author of over two dozen mystery novels, including the Shamus Award-winning *True Detectives* and the film novelization of *Dick Tracy*. Max has written the syndicated newspaper comic strip *Dick Tracy* since its creator, the late Chester Gould, retired in 1977. He is the co-creator of Ms. Tree and Wild Dog for DC and has also scripted Batman.

GERRY CONWAY

Gerry Conway was still a teenager when he published his first science-fiction novel and broke into comic-book writing soon after, in the early 1970s, for Marvel Comics. For Marvel, Gerry wrote virtually every character on their roster, including a long run on *Spider-Man*, as well as serving in various editorial capacities. For DC, Gerry has written almost as many features, including Batman, Hercules Unbound, Steel, Firestorm, Superman, and many others. Gerry currently writes for Marvel Comics while he pursues a successful career in Hollywood.

STEVE ENGLEHART

Steve Englehart has been writing comics for over twenty years, his work appearing in the top titles for both Marvel and DC Comics, including Batman, Superman, Green Lantern, *Fantastic Four*, *The Avengers*, *Master of Kung Fu*, and *Spider-Man*. Steve was also one of the pioneer creators to work in the independent comics field.

BILL FINGER

Bill Finger was one of the true innovative talents and legendary figures of the comics industry. He collaborated with Bob Kane on the creation of Batman and scripted the first two episodes of the Dark Knight's appearances in DETECTIVE COMICS. Bill went on to script features for many publishers, including Plastic Man (for Quality Comics), Green Lantern, Wildcat, Vigilante, Johnny Quick, Superman, Superboy, Blackhawk, Tomahawk, Robin, Challengers of the Unknown, Batman (in comic books and in the syndicated newspaper strip), as well as Captain America and ALL WINNERS COMICS (for Timely). Bill also wrote for radio and television, contributing scripts to *Mark Trail*, *77 Sunset Strip*, *The Roaring Twenties*, *Hawaiian Eye*, and, naturally enough, two episodes of the *Batman* TV program in 1966. He also wrote television commercials and co-wrote one feature film, the 1969 cult film *The Green Slime*. Bill Finger was still writing for DC Comics at the time of his death in 1974.

GARDNER FOX

As much as any writer, Gardner Fox helped create the tone and feel of the Batman stories of the 1960s. Gardner was an attorney who began his prolific and innovative second career as a writer in the late 1930s on Batman and went on to create such Golden Age classics as the original Flash, Hawkman, Starman, Doctor Fate, and the Justice Society of America. His influence extended throughout the 1950s and 1960s when, until his retirement from DC Comics in 1968, he created and/or wrote such memorable features as the Justice League of America, Adam Strange, The Atom, Hawkman, and, of course, Batman, all under the auspices of legendary comics editor Julius Schwartz. Until his death in 1986, Gardner Fox continued writing comics and novels. He published over 100 books in numerous genres, some under the pseudonyms of Jefferson Cooper and Bart Sommers, as well as many fantasy novels under his own name.

JOE GIELLA

Inker Joe Giella began his career in the 1940s as an inker for Hillman Publications and Timely Comics, the company that was to become Marvel in later years. Joe first worked for DC Comics in 1951 where, in the 1960s, his unique style of embellishment became associated with some of the company's greatest heroes, including Batman (over the work of penciller Sheldon Moldoff), The Flash (with artist Carmine Infantino), and The Atom (with penciller Gil Kane). Giella, who also pencilled and inked a run of the Batman syndicated newspaper strip during the 1960s, retired from comics in the early 1980s.

DICK GIORDANO

Dick Giordano was part of the creative team that, more than any other, helped change the face of comic books in the late 1960s and early 1970s. Along with writer Dennis O'Neil and penciller Neal Adams, Dick helped bring Batman back to his roots as a dark, brooding "creature of the night," and brought relevance to comics in the pages of GREEN LANTERN/GREEN ARROW. Dick began his career as an artist for Charlton Comics in 1952 and became the company's editor-in-chief in 1965. In that capacity, he revamped their line by adding an emphasis on such "action heroes" as The Question, Captain Atom, Thunderbolt, and The Blue Beetle (characters now published by DC Comics). In 1967, Dick came over to DC for a three-year stint as editor, bringing with him many of the talents who

GRANT
BREYFOGLE
SALE

would help shape the industry of the day, including Dennis O'Neil, Jim Aparo, and Steve Skeates. The winner of numerous industry awards, Dick continues to be a major influence in comics, both as one of the most respected artists in the business, as well as in the position of DC's Vice President-Editorial Director.

SID GREENE
Artist Sid Greene got his start in comics in 1941 and was soon drawing features for such publishing houses as Timely and Novelty. Sid came to DC in 1955, where he did the bulk of his work throughout the 1960s and 1970s, pencilling and/or inking a wide variety of genre stories and such features as Star Rovers, Johnny Peril, The Atom, Elongated Man, Hawkman, The Justice League of America, The Flash, Hourman, and, of course, The Batman. His credits for Marvel Comics from the late 1970s include *Ka-Zar* and *S.H.I.E.L.D.*

EDMOND HAMILTON
The late Ed Hamilton had a long and active career in both comics and prose fiction, beginning in the 1930s and continuing through the ensuing decades, until his death in the 1980s. During the 1940s, Ed wrote for numerous comic book companies, including scripts for such features as Batman, Superman, and Green Lantern. Among his most well known and best regarded work for DC were his efforts on the cult favorite Legion of Super-Heroes. Ed Hamilton was also the author of numerous pulp stories and science-fiction novels.

FRANCE EDDIE HERRON
Eddie Herron was one of the mainstay DC writers of the 1940s, 1950s, and 1960s, with a list of credits that includes a wide variety of characters and genres. Eddie's work appeared extensively in the science fiction, mystery, and super-hero titles, including MYSTERY IN SPACE, STRANGE ADVENTURES, SUPERMAN, and, of course, BATMAN.

BRUCE JONES
Bruce Jones is both a writer and accomplished artist whose work has appeared in the pages of numerous DC, Marvel, and independently published comic books. In addition to his writing credits on the Catwoman tales in BATMAN, Bruce's work has also appeared in Marvel's *Ka-Zar*.

BOB KANE
Bob Kane created Batman in 1939 after three years spent pencilling and inking comic book features for a variety of publishers, including the legendary Eisner/Iger Studios, as well as a stint working on the Betty Boop animated cartoons for the Fleischer Studios. Bob contributed most of the pencilling and cover art, as well as significant amounts of inking, to the early years of the Batman feature in DETECTIVE COMICS and BATMAN. In 1943, Bob discontinued most of his comic book work to concentrate his talents on the daily syndicated newspaper strip. He remained connected with the Batman comic book until 1968. During the 1960s, Bob also created the animated cartoon series, *Courageous Cat & Minute Mouse* and *Cool McCool*. Since the late 1960s, Bob Kane has been involved in numerous one-man art shows in galleries and museums nationwide, as well as the creation of limited-edition lithographs. Now living in California, Bob served as a consultant on the 1989 movie *Batman* and the current *Batman Returns*.

PABLO MARCOS
The work of artist Pablo Marcos has appeared in the comics of numerous publishers in America and abroad for many years. As either penciller or inker, he has worked for DC, Marvel, Atlas, and other publishers on such features as Batman, Conan, Star Trek, Green Arrow, and Warlord. Pablo's work currently appears in many titles for DC.

SHELDON MOLDOFF
Sheldon Moldoff, who began his career at DC Comics in 1938, came to prominence in comics in the early 1940s with his work on the Hawkman feature in FLASH COMICS under the signature "Shelly." Shelly's early style, reminiscent of the work of Alex Raymond and Hal Foster, was distinctive in its own right, earning him work on a variety of adventure and humor features for DC and other publishers throughout the 1940s and 1950s. In 1943, Shelly began what was to be a 25-year association with the Batman feature in both BATMAN and DETEC-

TIVE COMICS, and his style as both penciller and inker was so dominant, he served to define the look and style of the Batman feature for the duration of his run. Shelly left comics in the late 1960s to work on animation storyboards for such cartoon series as *Courageous Cat & Minute Mouse* and *Cool McCool*.

DON NEWTON

Don Newton was one of the best known and most popular artists in comic book fandom in the late 1960s and early 1970s before turning professional for Charlton Comics, where his work appeared in their horror titles and in *The Phantom*. Don began working at DC Comics soon after as the penciller of SHAZAM!, The Original Captain Marvel. He also had a long run as the penciller of Batman in BATMAN and DETECTIVE COMICS, as well as on Aquaman, DC COMICS PRESENTS, and Green Lantern Corps. Don was still working for DC at the time of his death in the mid-1980s.

IRV NOVICK

Irv Novick began his comic book career at the dawn of the Golden Age. Among his earliest work was the first appearance of The Shield in 1940 for MLJ Magazines, later Archie Comics. Irv was also the artist on Steel Sterling and other features for MLJ and numerous other publishers. He later came to work for DC Comics, working on stories for the war anthologies and features, including CAPTAIN STORM, and, later, on super-hero titles. During the 1960s, Irv's work was featured in such titles as BATMAN and DETECTIVE COMICS. He was later to have a long run as penciller on THE FLASH.

DENNIS O'NEIL

Dennis O'Neil was a journalist who broke into comic books in 1965 at Marvel Comics, where he worked on such features as Millie the Model and The Two-Gun Kid before moving over to Charlton Comics under editorial director Dick Giordano. At Charlton he wrote a variety of features under the pseudonym "Sergius O'Shaunessey," a name he later took with him when he moved over to DC Comics in 1967, accompanying Dick Giordano on his move to the company. Denny scripted several features at his new creative home, including Justice League of America, Wonder Woman, Bat Lash, Superman, The Creeper, and Captain Marvel. Denny is best remembered for his groundbreaking work in returning the Batman to his dark and gritty roots as a "creature of the night" with artists Neal Adams and Giordano and, with that same team, bringing the touch of realism and relevance to the pages of GREEN LANTERN/GREEN ARROW. After a stint as a writer and editor at Marvel Comics, Denny returned to DC, where he wrote The Question, THE BATMAN movie adaptation, and is the editor of the Batman line of comics.

CHARLES PARIS

Inker Charles Paris began his career inking Mort Meskin on the Johnny Quick and Vigilante features for DC in the 1940s, but he is best known for his work on Batman, a feature he inked from 1947 through 1964 over such pencillers as Jack Burnley, Fred Ray, Sheldon Moldoff, and Dick Sprang. After Batman (including many of the Batman Sunday newspaper strips of the 1940s), Charlie went on to ink other DC features, including Metamorpho, many issues of THE BRAVE AND THE BOLD, including the first appearance of the Teen Titans. Charlie retired from comics in 1968 to travel and paint.

JERRY ROBINSON

Jerry Robinson was a 17-year-old about to start college when he met Batman creator and artist Bob Kane at a summer resort, a chance meeting that resulted in a career that persists to this day. Jerry began as Kane's assistant, and soon graduated to both pencilling and inking the feature. Among his many contributions to the Batman mythos of the 1940s was a definition of the strip's look and style, the creation of the visual look of the Joker, and the naming of Robin, the Boy Wonder. After leaving Batman, Robinson went on to work on Vigilante and Johnny Quick for DC, the Green Hornet and other features for Harvey Comics, and a variety of features for other publishers, including Atlas and Western Publishing. In 1961, he began writing and drawing political and social commentary strips for the Chicago Tribune-New York News Syndicate and *Classroom Fluffs and Flubs* for *The New York Daily News*. Since 1977, Jerry has headed the Cartoonists and Writers Syndicate, which syndicates cartoons and features to 40 countries around the world.

MARSHALL ROGERS

A former architecture student, Marshall Rogers began working at DC in the mid-1970s, pencilling a variety of mystery and super-hero short stories. He quickly rose to artistic prominence with his assignment to the Batman feature in DETECTIVE COMICS with writer Steve Englehart and inker Terry Austin, a run many fans consider the definitive portrayal of the Dark Knight.

GEORGE ROUSSOS

George Roussos began working as an art assistant to Batman creator Bob Kane in 1940, inking backgrounds and doing lettering on the strip. George eventually began inking Batman over such pencillers as Dick Sprang, and was soon pencilling on his own for other DC features, including Air Wave. George was also an innovative color artist, contributing his sense of color to hundreds of stories over the years. George left DC for Marvel Comics in 1972 where he still works as cover colorist.

ALVIN SCHWARTZ

Writer Alvin Schwartz had his first story published when he was 12 and was hooked for life, his poetry appearing in literary magazines while he was still a high school student. Schwartz began writing for comics in 1941 for Street and Smith Publications and came over to DC a short time later after meeting DC editor Sheldon Mayer. Alvin wrote for such features as Green Arrow, The Newsboy Legion, Wonder Woman, and the Flash, as well as Captain Marvel stories for Fawcett Comics. In addition to these stories, he also wrote numerous continuities for the 1940s Batman syndicated strip as well as the comic books, and such features as Aquaman, Slam Bradley, A Date with Judy, Star-Spangled Kid, Superman, Superboy, the Superman newspaper strip, and many others. He also wrote extensively outside of comic books, including novels under his own name and the name Robert W. Tracy. Alvin Schwartz left comic books in the late 1950s to set up the consulting firm Human Factors Analysis.

LEW SAYRE SCHWARTZ

During the 1950s, Lew Sayre Schwartz was one of numerous Batman artists who served to fill the large demand for material starring the Caped Crusader and his Boy Wonder sidekick in DETECTIVE COMICS, BATMAN, and WORLD'S FINEST COMICS.

DICK SPRANG

Dick Sprang was one of the earliest artists hired by DC to draw Batman in the early 1940s when the demand for stories outstripped Dark Knight creator Bob Kane's studio's ability to produce material. Dick's dynamic, energetic style was unique among all the Batman "ghost" artists, and his 25-year run on the Batman titles (with regular forays into the pages of WORLD'S FINEST COMICS) helped define the look of the character throughout the 1950s. Dick retired from comics freelancing in 1961 and currently lives in Arizona where, in between creating giant-sized full-color painting reproductions of his famous Batman covers from the 1940s and 1950s, he contributes the occasional illustration or cover to DC.

CHIC STONE

Inker Chic Stone's credits date back to the 1950s and the American Comic Group. His work gained recognition in the pages of the Marvel Comics of the early 1960s when it appeared over such pencillers as Jack Kirby and Don Heck. Chic was also an accomplished penciller, his work appearing in issues of many Marvel Comics, as well as at DC on Batman.

TREVOR VON EEDEN

Trevor Von Eeden began his pencilling career at DC Comics while still a high school student in the mid-1970s when he was picked to draw Black Lightning. Trevor has continued drawing since, with work appearing in a number of titles for DC, including the Catwoman feature in BATMAN and his recent work on Black Canary and Green Arrow.

DAVE STEVENS

(Paul Kupperberg is an Editor at DC Comics and a member of its Development Group.)